A Children's Songbook
Companion
Artbook

Illustrated by
Nina Grover

A Children's Songbook Companion Artbook
This work is not an official publication of The Church of Jesus Christ of Latter-day Saints.

Copyright © 1995 by Aspen Books
All rights reserved.

Limited permission is granted to the purchaser to copy and/or enlarge the artwork, charts, and images provided in this book for personal use only, to enhance instruction and presentation of the materials. Permission to copy is strictly limited to the owner of *A Children's Songbook Companion Artbook* and not for larger audiences or organizations. Standard copyrights prohibit the reproduction of complete sections of this work.

Printed in the United States of America
10 9 8 7 6 5 4 3 2 1

Artbook Design by Robert Davis.
Based on design of *A Children's Songbook Companion* by Becky Porter.

Using the Artbook

Twenty-five years of involvement with children has strengthened Nina Grover's deeply held conviction that children learn better when they are able to both see and hear an idea. The original art work she produced for *A Children's Songbook Companion* is unique, sensitive, and appealing—worthy to be enlarged and made even more usable in a clip art volume such as this. Permission to enlarge each drawing as needed for teaching is given with the purchase of this book.

The Illustrations

- are **simple** and **reproducible**. The images are meant for your use as you prepare visuals to aid in teaching children.
- **include many subjects** that are relatively hard to find in clear simple images that children readily identify.
- **reflect an appropriate reverence** for the sacred ideas expressed in gospel-theme songs. Animation has a significant presence in children's lives today, but using stylization may cause children to view an image as "just for fun" and not to be taken seriously. For that reason Nina avoided cartoon-type images.
- are as **timeless** as possible. Most of the images can be used indefinitely without modification. Feel free to update clothing and hairstyles.
- **compatible** throughout the book so that you may mix and match to create your own presentation ideas.

How to Use the Illustrations in This Book:

Please refer to the first section of *A Children's Songbook Companion* for a variety of possible ways to use these materials. The ideas printed there will help you find the most effective and creative ways to use them to meet your particular needs.

Enlarging

With today's copier technology it is possible to enlarge or reduce an image to any size you need. However, please be aware that as you enlarge a smaller image the line quality of the image will become increasingly rough as the image becomes larger. (This is one reason that the larger images in this *Artbook* will be more helpful to you than the smaller ones in the *Companion*.) If you want to make an extremely large picture, it will look better if you use an opaque projector and trace the image rather than making multiple enlargements on a copier. Schools and libraries, including some ward and stake libraries, have these projectors and are often willing to let you use them.

Coloring

Choose from the many options according to the look you wish to achieve.

- You will usually want to outline the image in black, then color vividly.
- Colored pencils are good for shading.
- Markers give a very bright look.
- Crayons and colored pencils can be made to look soft or bright. Look for soft colored pencils for ease of use and for brighter colors.

- Pastels or chalk are good for when you have a large image to color. Set with a spray fixative or hairspray.
- Relatively dry paint such as tempura or designers gauche can be used, but make a pretest to be sure they will not wrinkle your paper.

For large areas you may find it faster to reproduce an image on colored paper and cut it out, rather than color it. Try:

- Construction paper. Copy stores have both bright and soft colors and good flesh-toned papers for faces, hands, and legs. They will often sell sheets singly—more economical when you need only a small number.
- Craft paper (especially good for really large images)
- Gift wrapping papers
- Wallpaper remnants

Patterned or plain fabrics also work well for large areas. Mix a combination of different coloring mediums to create your own special look.

Mounting

Mount black-and-white images on colored boards.
Mount pictures on patterned backgrounds made by gluing gift wrap or wallpaper on posterboard.
Mix solids and patterns for interesting looks.
Glue:

- Use rubber cement-based glues or gluesticks to mount any visual made of paper. (Water-based glues will cause the paper to wrinkle.)
- A heavy craft glue will work for fabrics.
- Hot glue from glue guns is best if you are attaching heavier objects such as buttons, moveable eyes, or little mirrors to your visual.

Lettering

To make lettering easier, try using stencils. Sizes up to 4 inches high are readily available. You can trace these onto colored or patterned paper, cut them out, and paste them into place. Another option is to use an opaque projector to enlarge a phrase or title to the size you need, then trace.

Remember two general rules about lettering:

- Avoid lettering in all caps. Children read and decipher upper- and lowercase lettering much easier than all capital letters.
- Space letters visually. Trust your eyes, not your ruler! The angles of the letters vary, and so must the spaces in order for them to look right.

Preserving Your Hard Work

A great visual deserves to last a long time. Cover with clear contact paper or have it laminated. (Many libraries have facilities where you can laminate them yourself.) A heavy coat of spray fixative is another way to help hand-colored pictures last. Investing in a large art storage pouch is also advisable so that your visuals stay wrinkle free and accessible.

Songbook 2-3

I AM A CHILD OF GOD

5

I LIVED IN HEAVEN

Songbook 4

Songbook 7

I THANK THEE DEAR FATHER

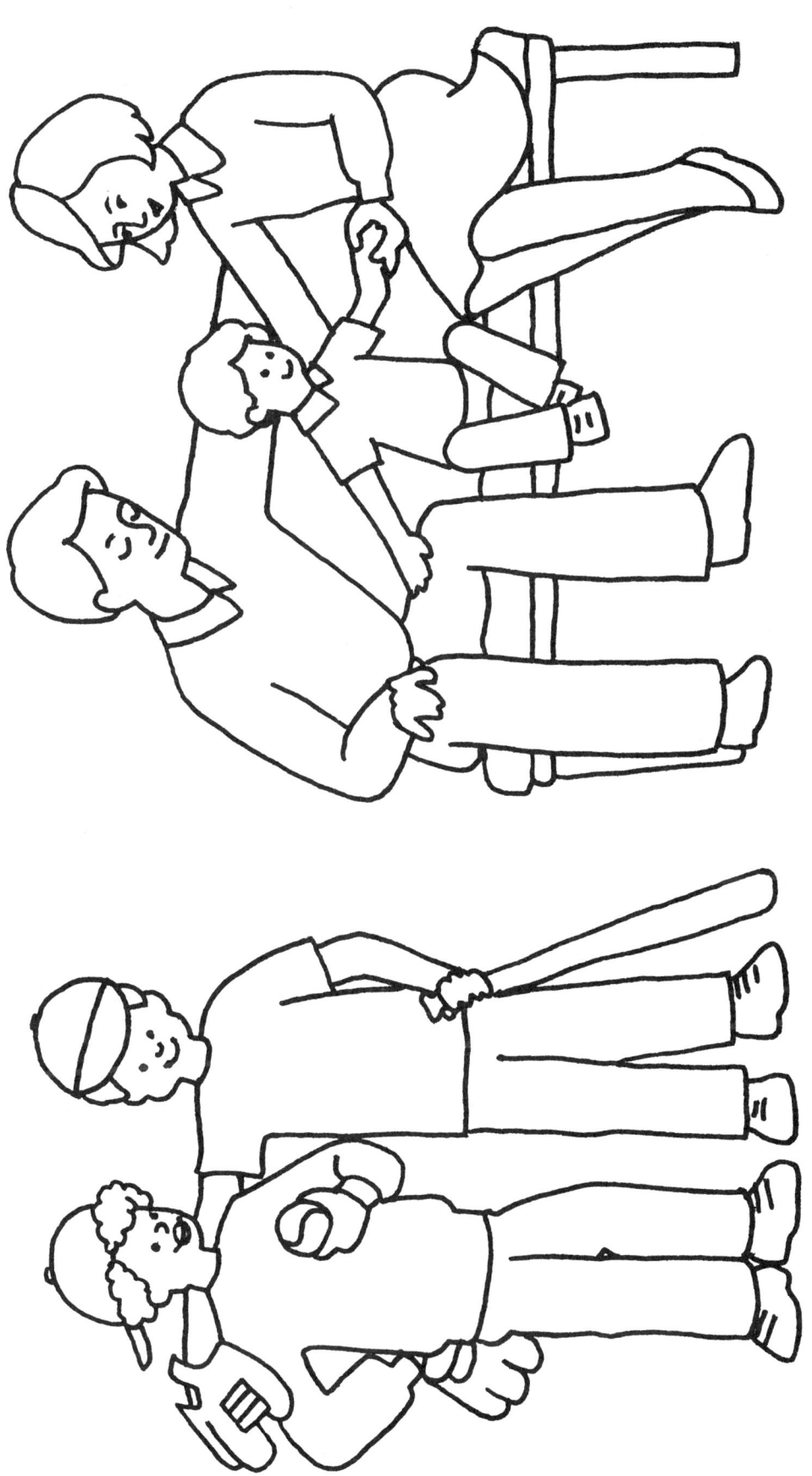

FATHER, WE THANK THEE FOR THE NIGHT

Songbook 8

Songbook 11

I'M THANKFUL TO BE ME

I PRAY IN FAITH

Songbook
14

10

Songbook 16-17

CHILDREN ALL OVER THE WORLD

11

I NEED MY HEAVENLY FATHER

Songbook 18

Songbook 20

A SONG OF THANKS

13

FOR HEALTH AND STRENGTH

Songbook 21

Songbook 22

A PRAYER SONG

15

A PRAYER

Songbook 22

16

Songbook
23

FATHER UP ABOVE

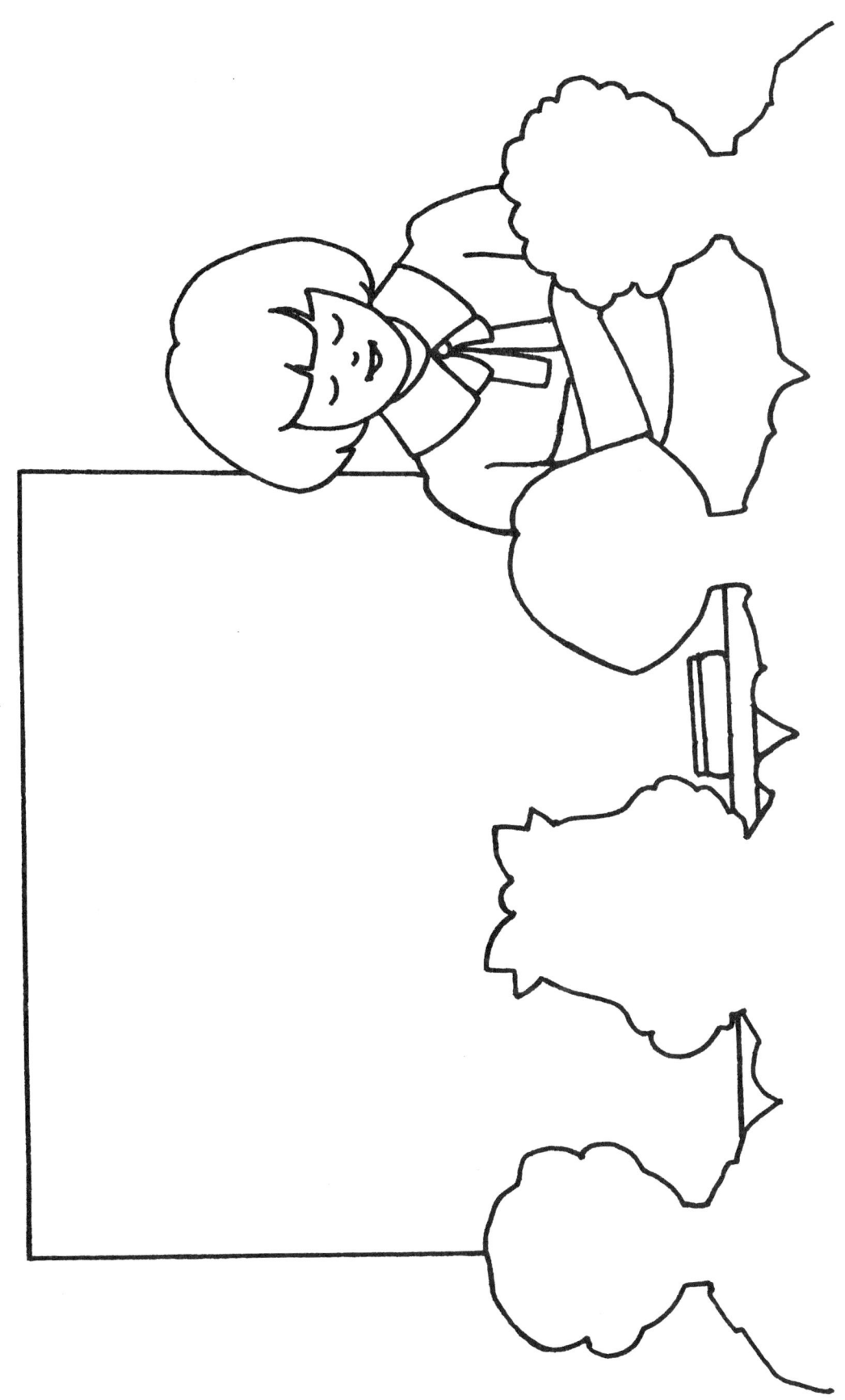

17

I LOVE TO PRAY

Songbook 25

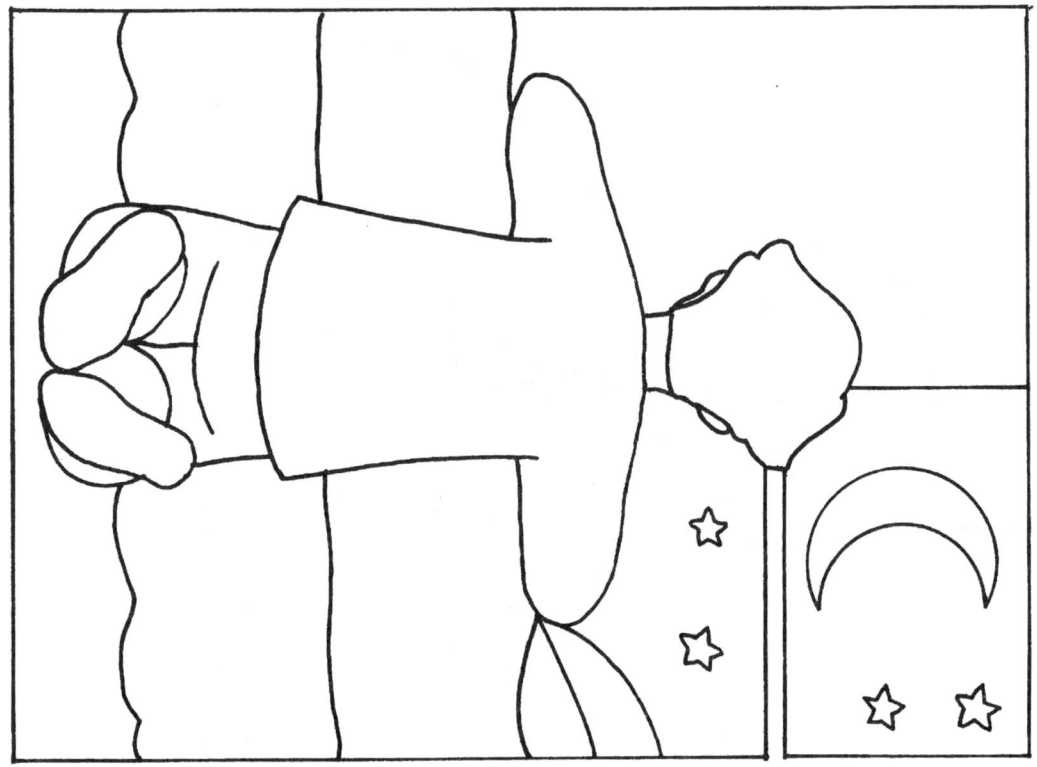

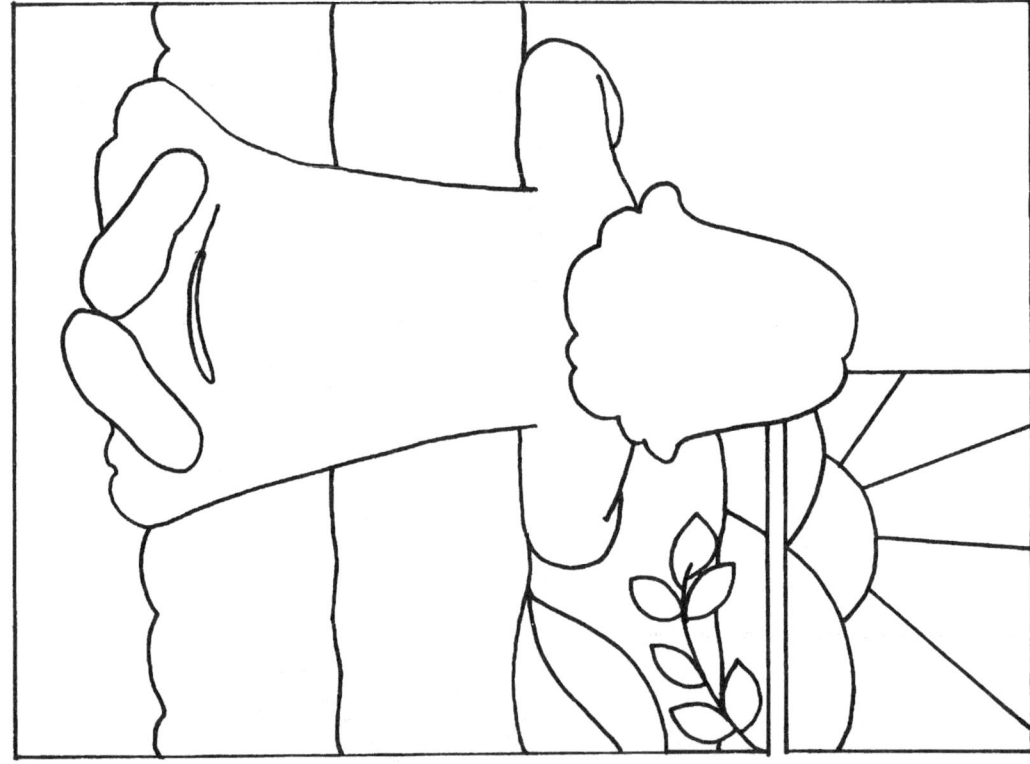

REVERENTLY, QUIETLY

REVERENCE

Songbook
27

Songbook 27

WE ARE REVERENT

21

WE ARE REVERENT

Songbook 27

Songbook 27

WE ARE REVERENT

WE ARE REVERENT

Songbook 27

Songbook 28

I WANT TO BE REVERENT

FATHER, I WILL REVERENT BE

Songbook 29

26

Songbook 30

THIS IS GOD'S HOUSE

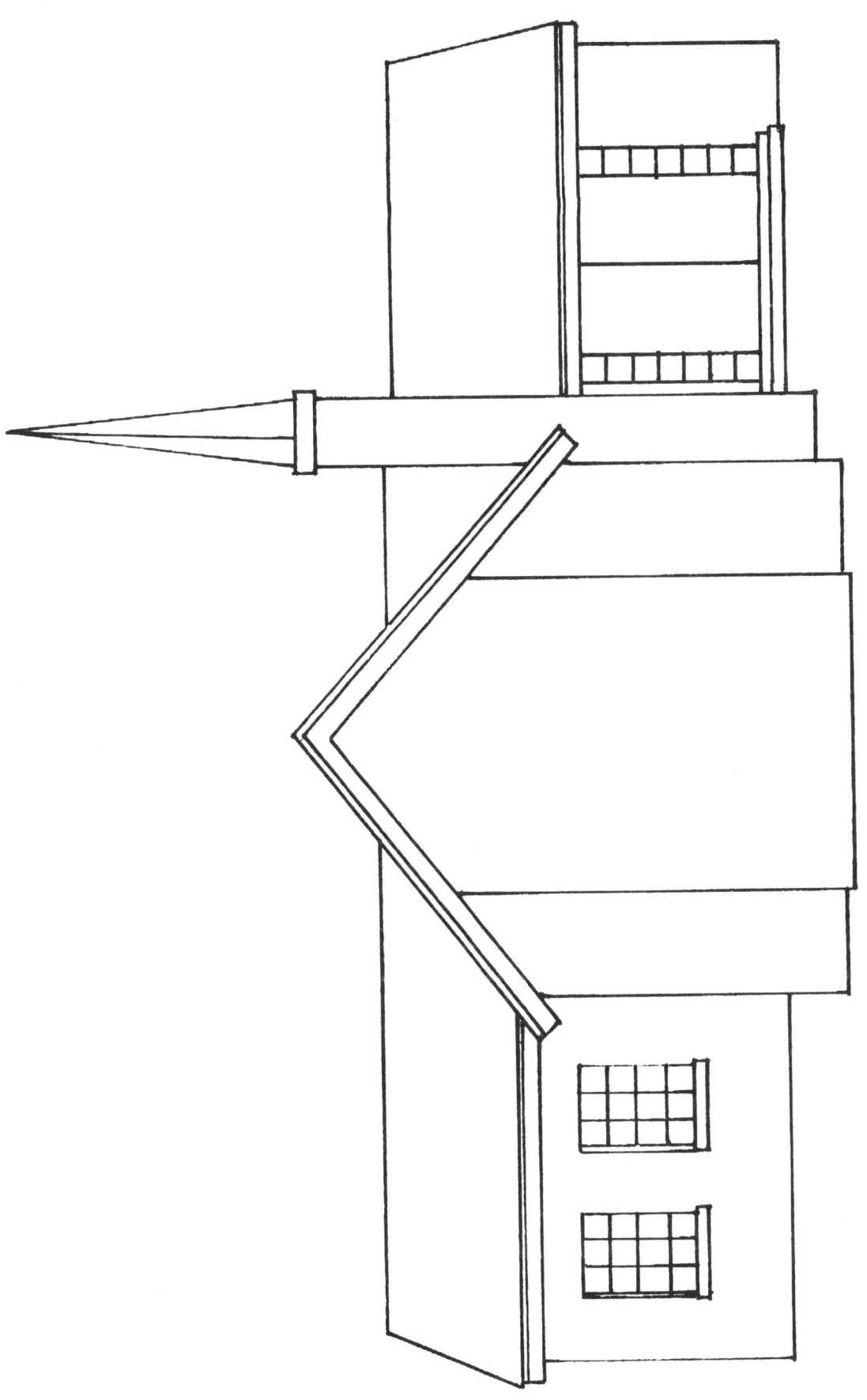

REVERENCE IS LOVE

Songbook 31

28

Songbook 36

SAMUEL TELLS OF THE BABY JESUS

WHEN JOSEPH WENT TO BETHLEHEM

Songbook
38-39

30

Songbook 38-39

WHEN JOSEPH WENT TO BETHLEHEM

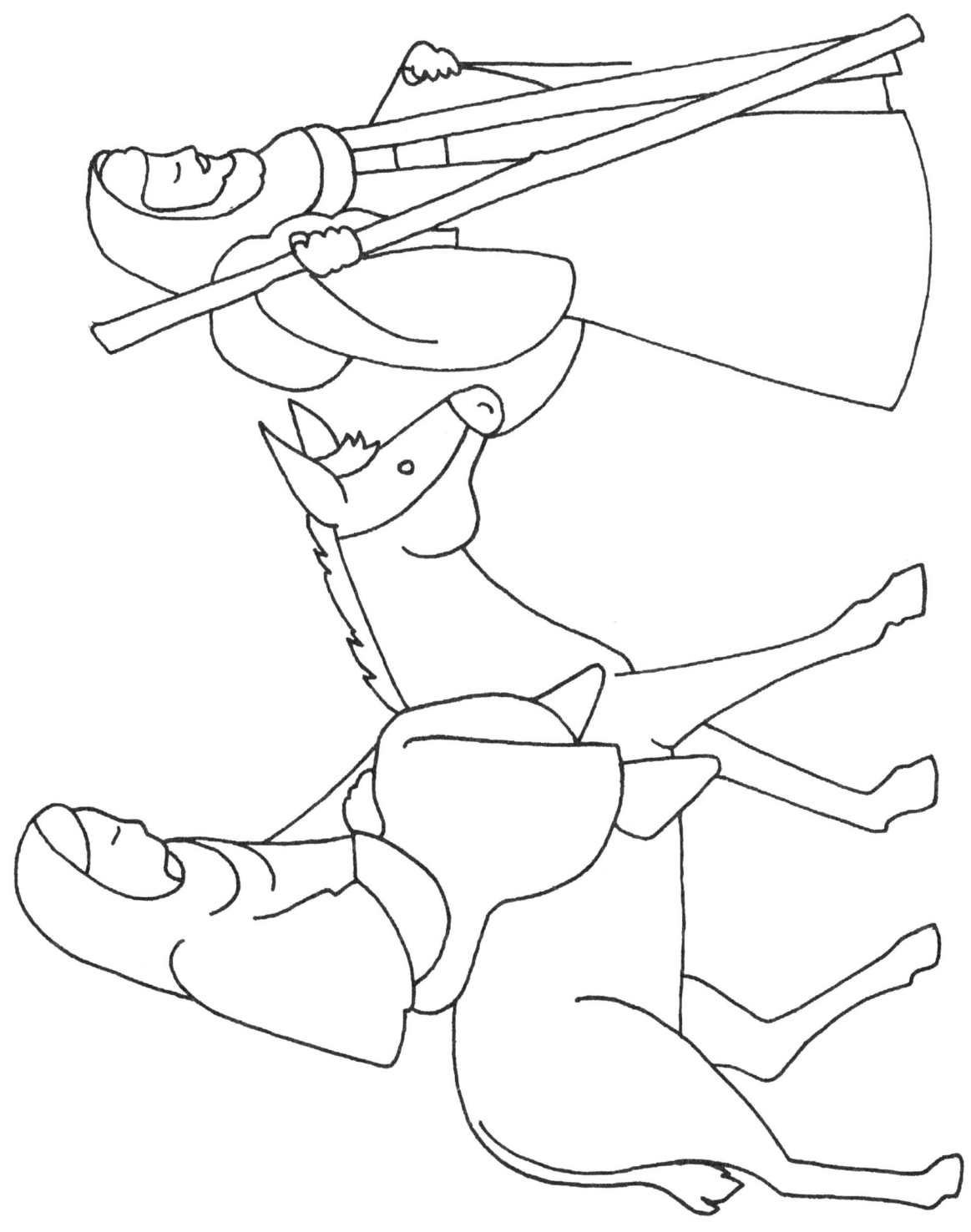

31

LITTLE JESUS

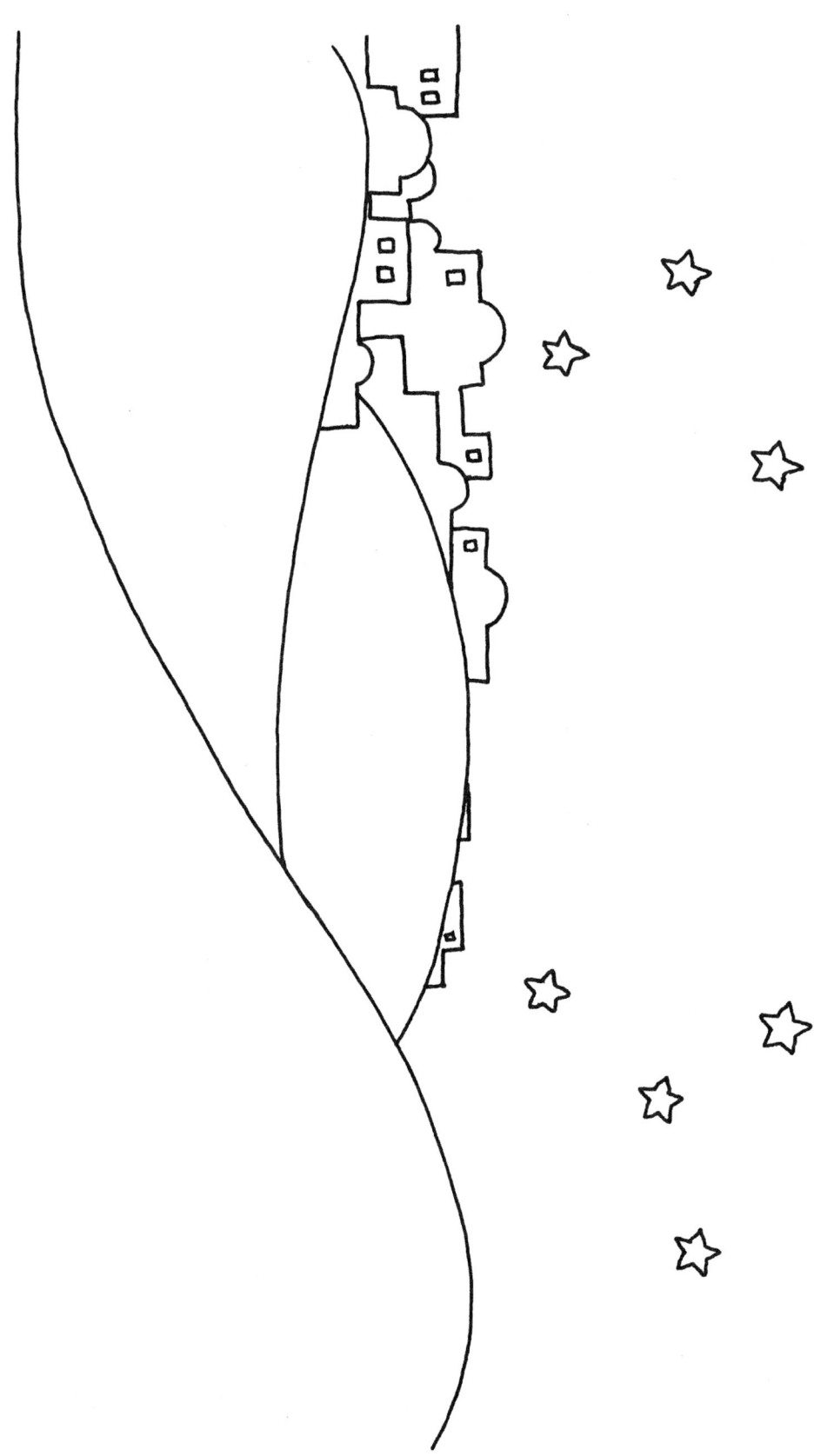

Songbook
39

LITTLE JESUS

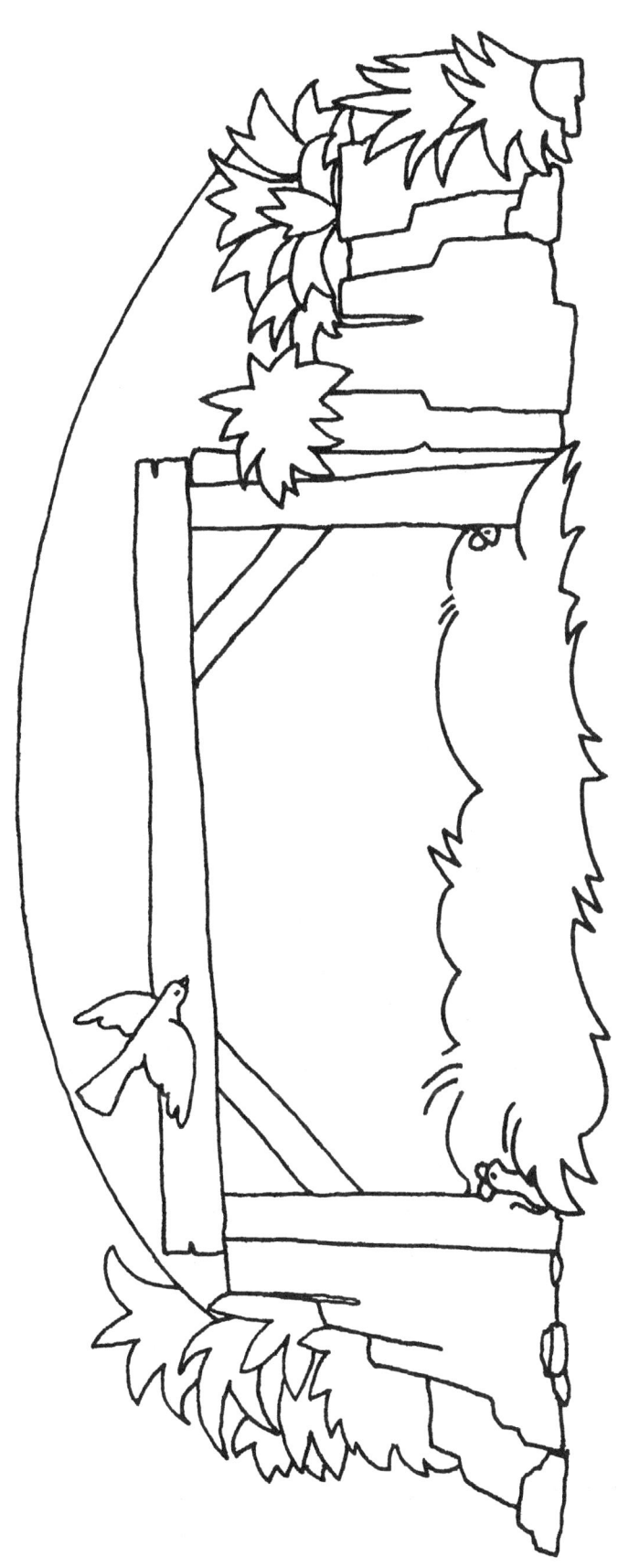

33

THERE WAS STARLIGHT ON THE HILLSIDE

Songbook 40

34

Songbook 40

THE SHEPHERD'S CAROL

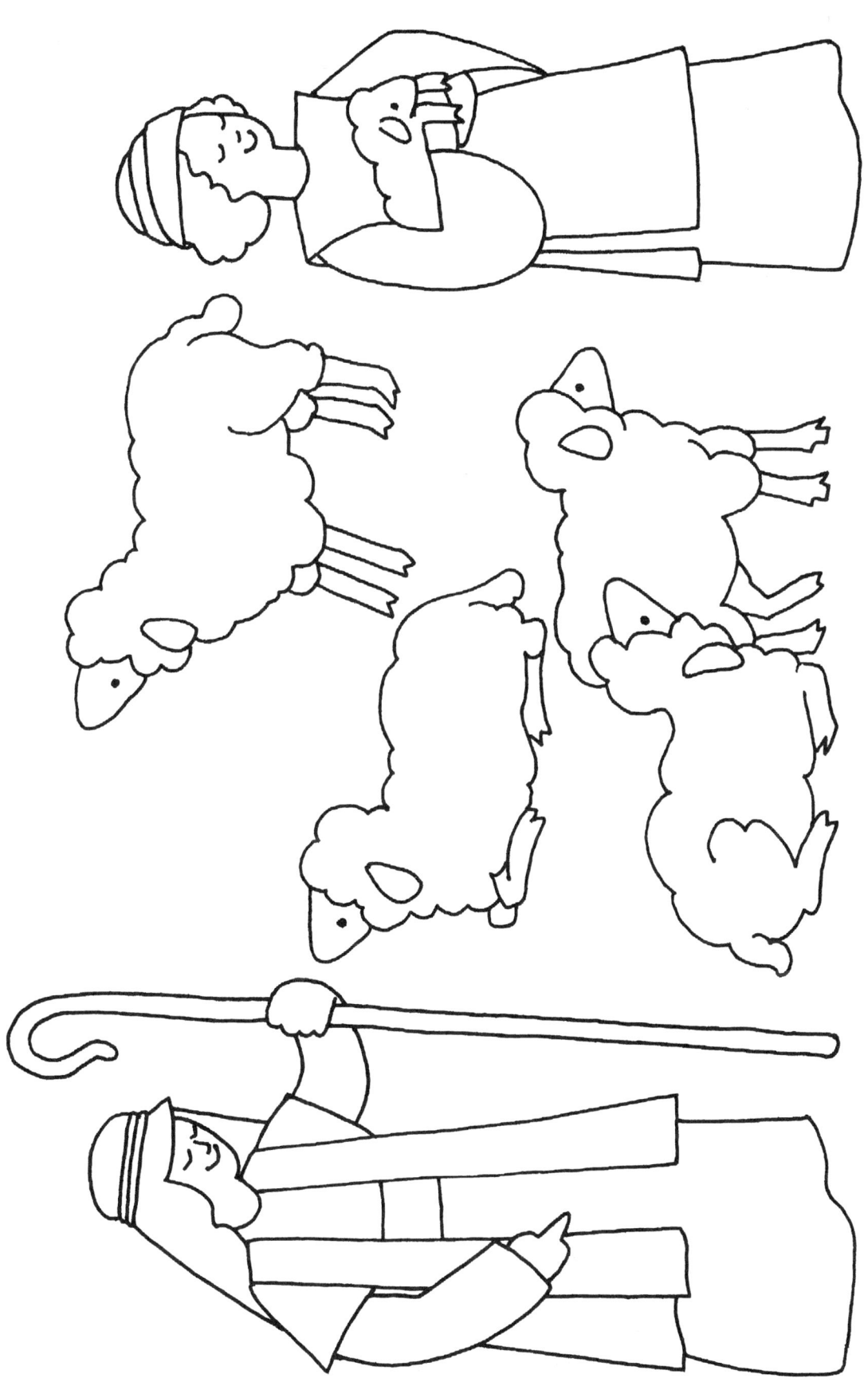

35

ONCE WITHIN A LOWLY STABLE

Songbook 41

Songbook
42-43

AWAY IN A MANGER

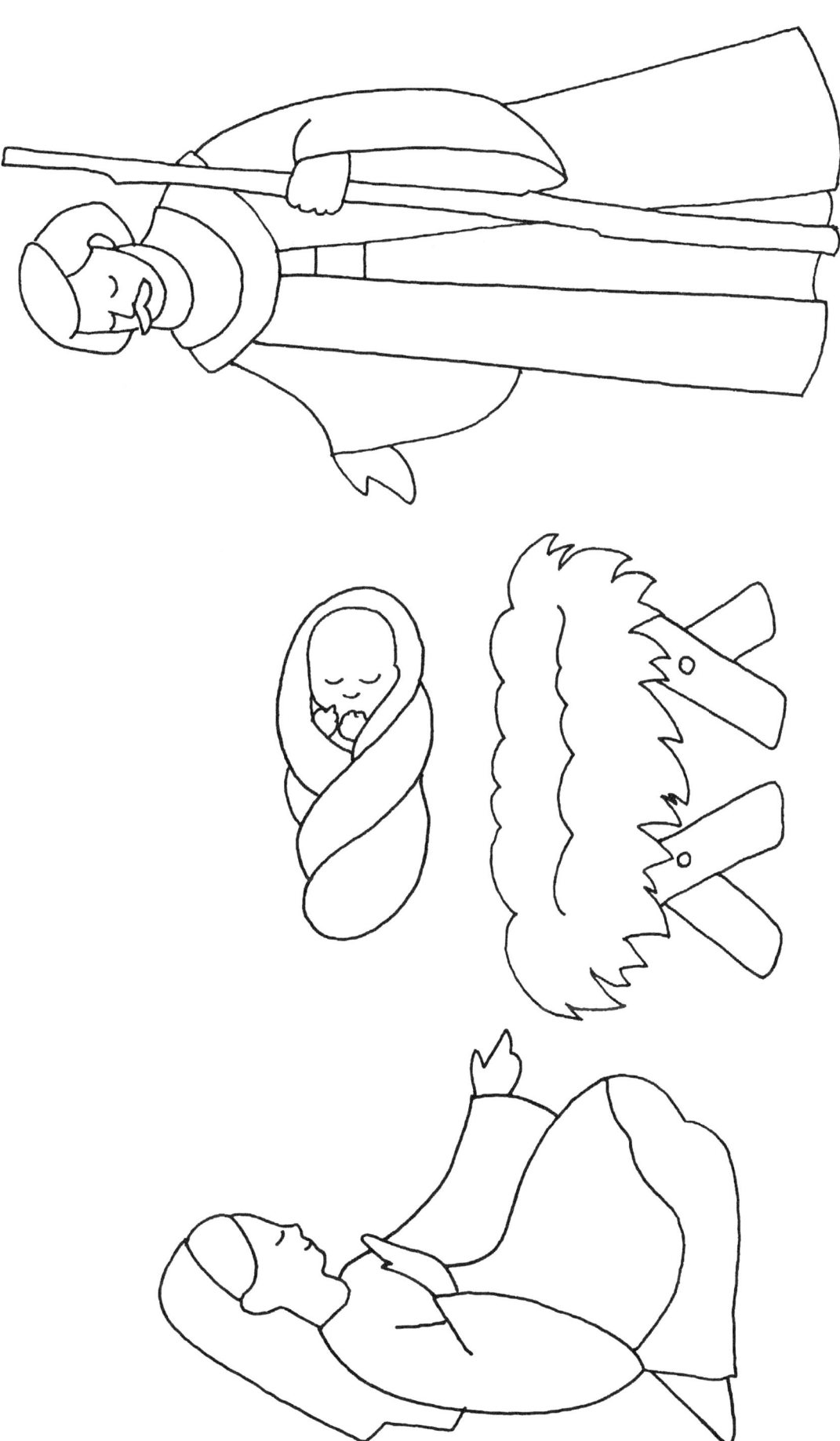

37

MARY'S LULLABY

Songbook
44-45

38

Songbook 46

WHO IS THE CHILD?

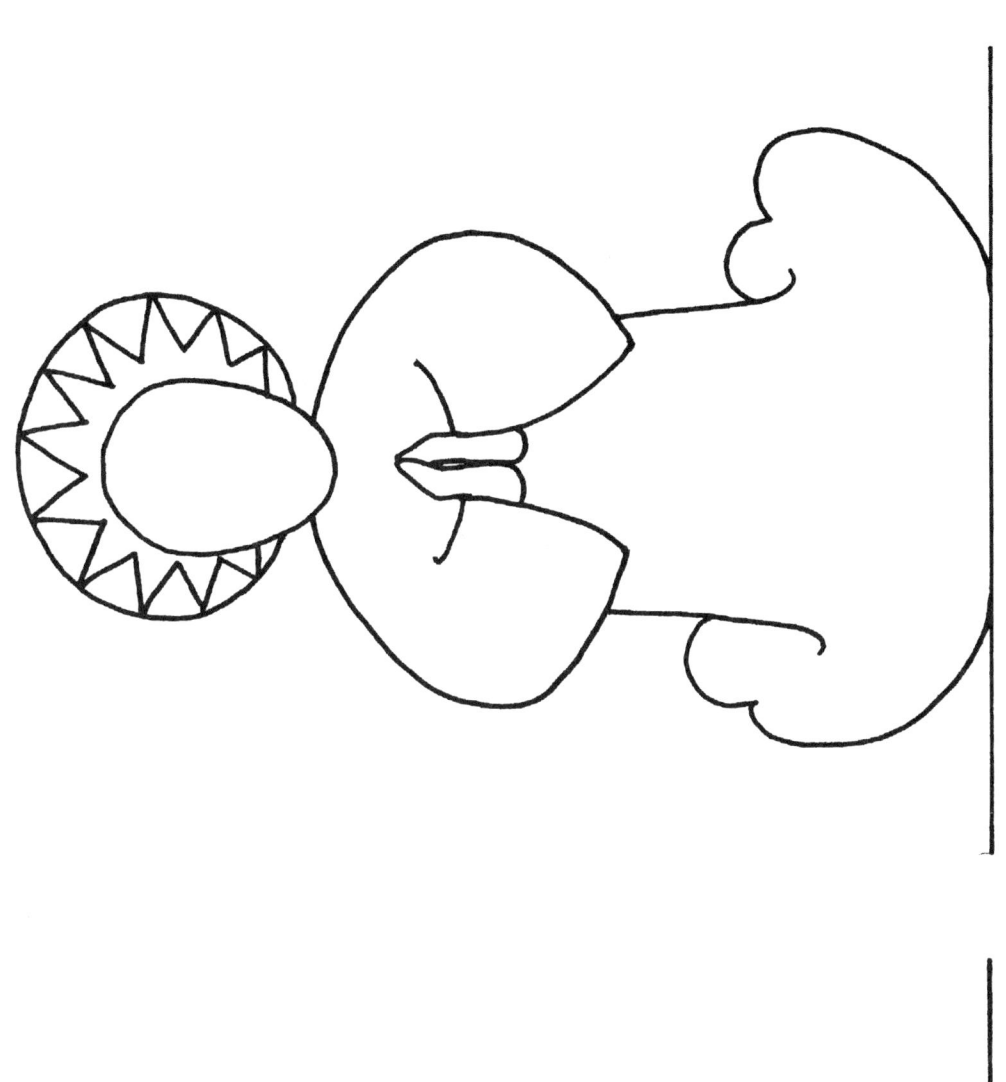
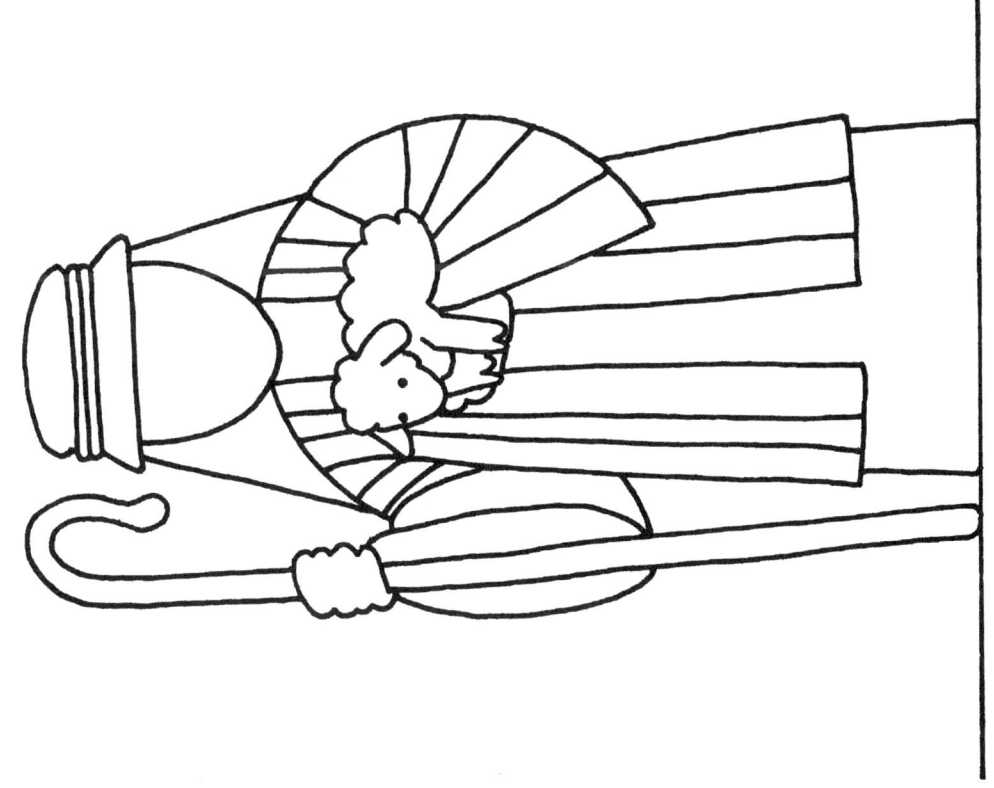

WHO IS THE CHILD?

Songbook 46

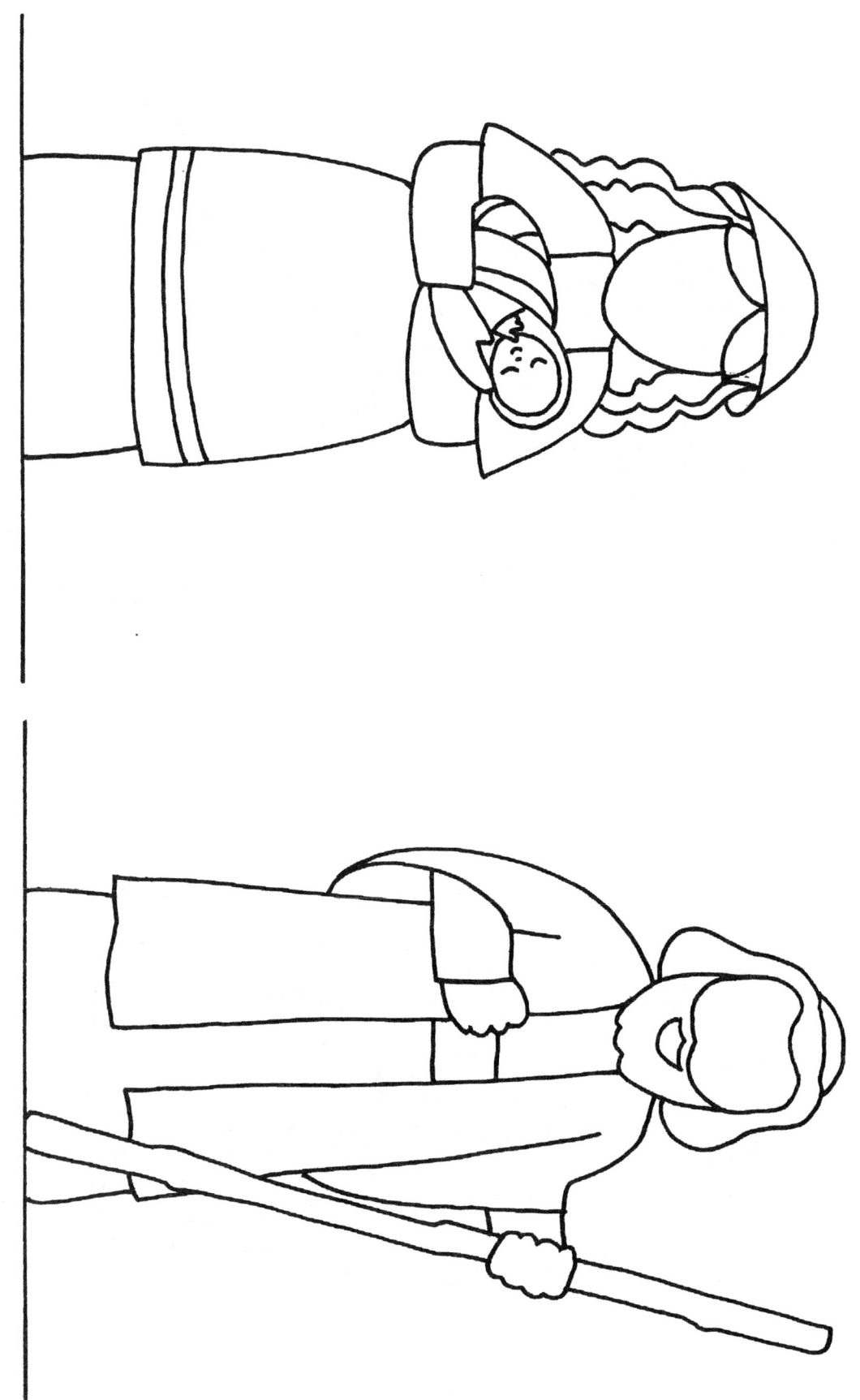

Songbook 48-49

OH, HUSH THEE, MY BABY

41

HAVE A VERY MERRY CHRISTMAS!

Songbook 51

THE NATIVITY SONG

Songbook 52-53

43

JESUS ONCE WAS A LITTLE CHILD

Songbook 55

Songbook 55

JESUS ONCE WAS A LITTLE CHILD

LITTLE LAMBS SO WHITE AND FAIR

Songbook 58

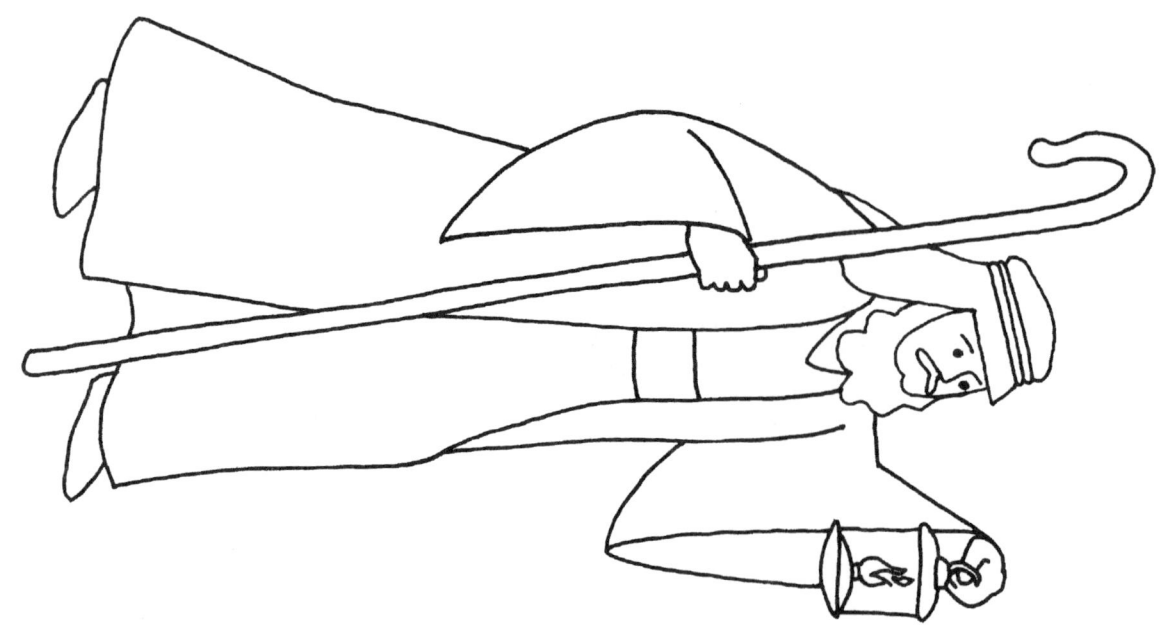

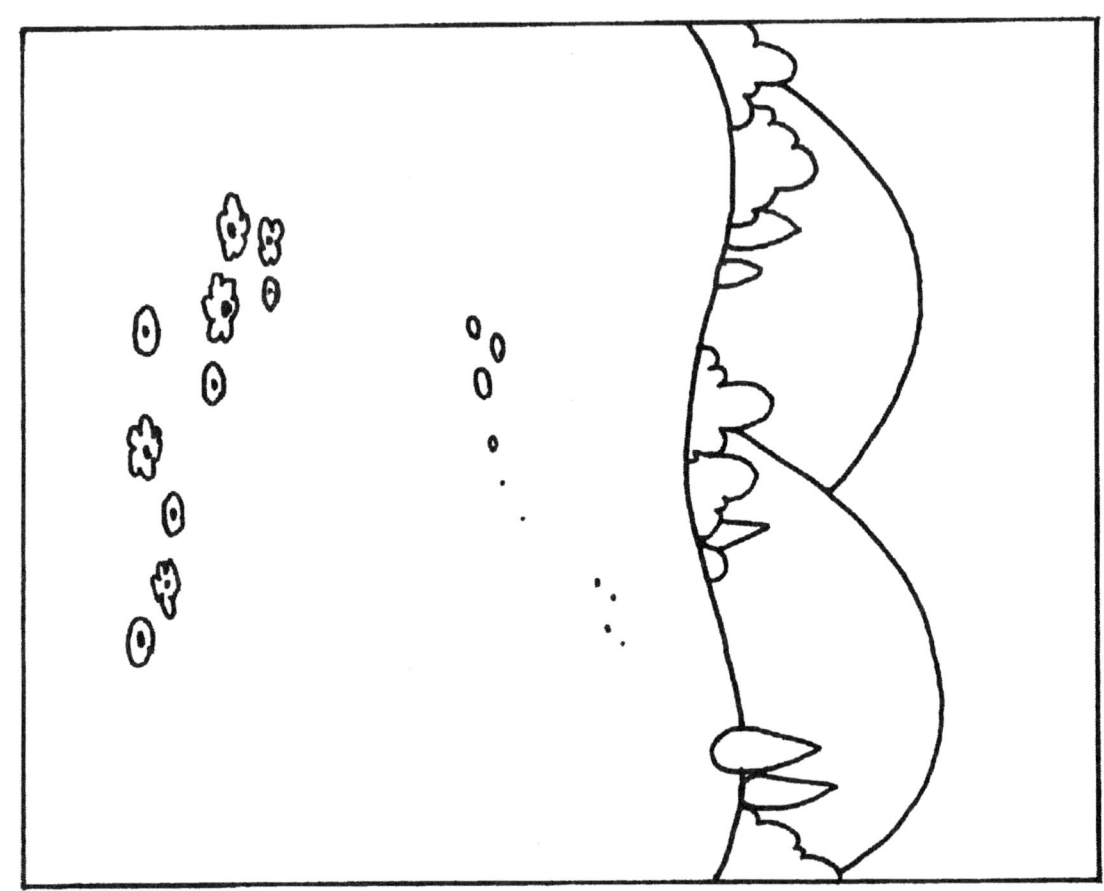

Songbook 58

JESUS IS OUR LOVING FRIEND

JESUS LOVED THE LITTLE CHILDREN

Songbook 59

Songbook 61

JESUS SAID LOVE EVERYONE

49

HE DIED THAT WE MIGHT LIVE AGAIN

Songbook 65

Songbook
66-67

HOSANNA

51

THE SACRAMENT

Songbook 72

Songbook 73

BEFORE I TAKE THE SACRAMENT

53

HELP US, O GOD, TO UNDERSTAND

Songbook 73

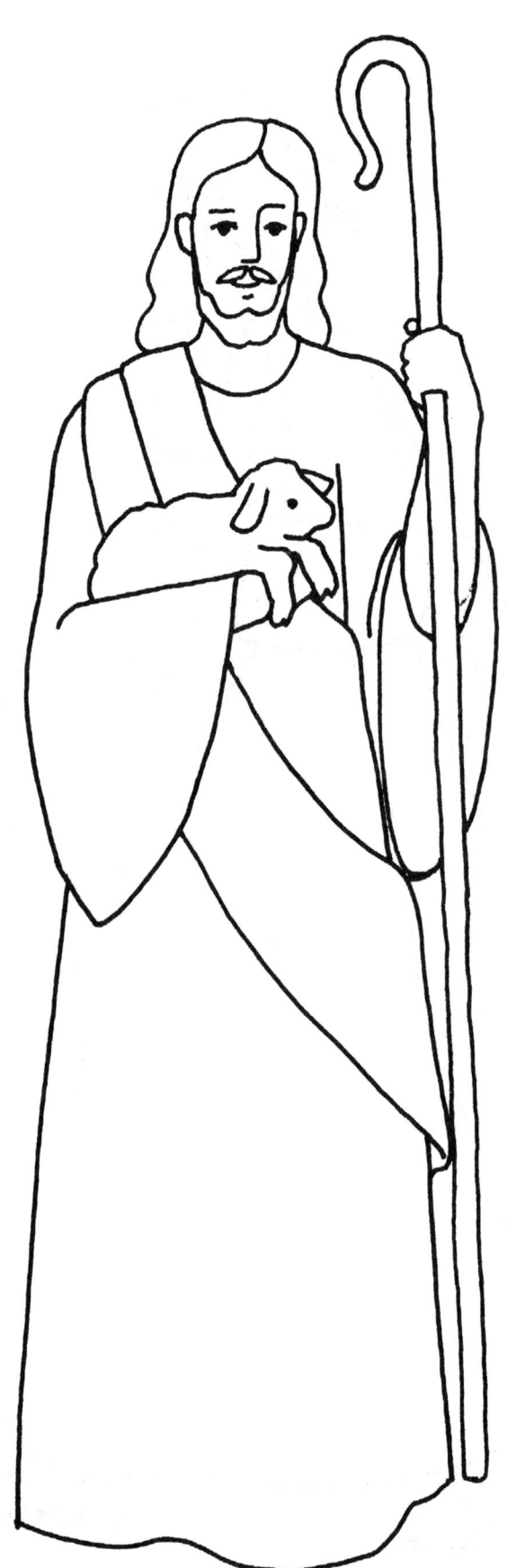

Songbook 76

THIS IS MY BELOVED SON

55

WHEN HE COMES AGAIN

Songbook 82-83

Songbook 86

THE GOLDEN PLATES

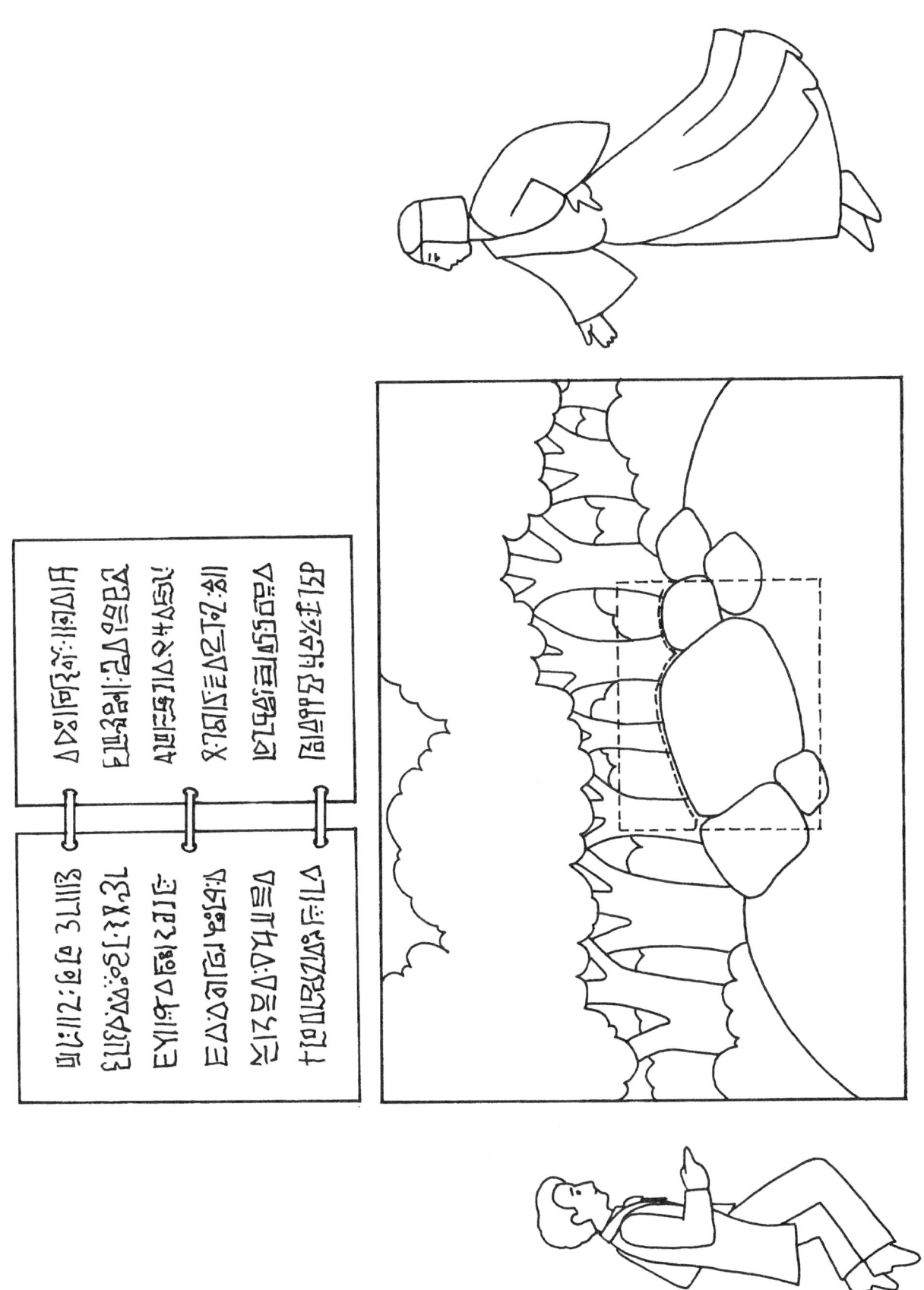

57

THE SACRED GROVE

Songbook 87

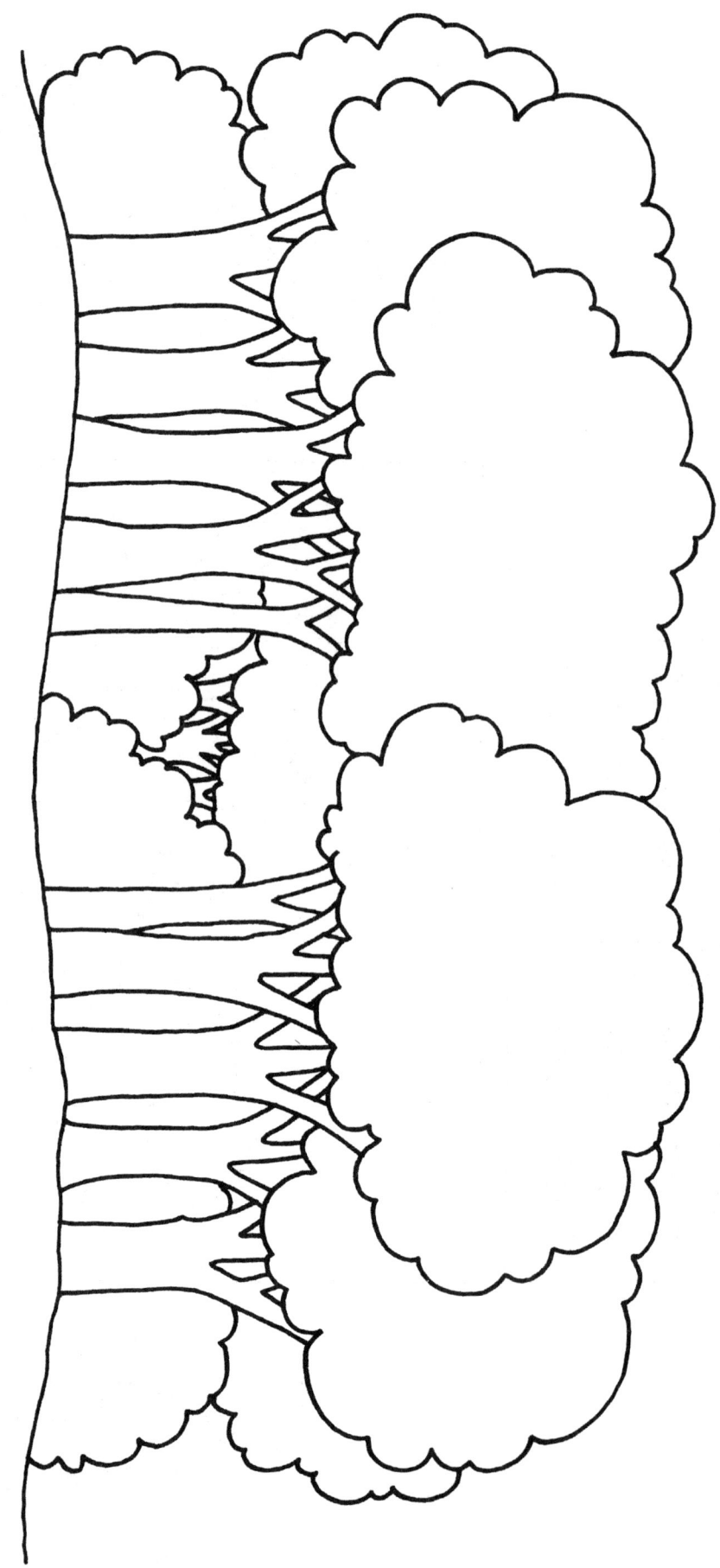

Songbook 87

THE SACRED GROVE

59

THE PRIESTHOOD IS RESTORED

Songbook 89

Songbook
90-91

TRUTH FROM ELIJAH

THE HEARTS OF THE CHILDREN

Songbook 92-93

Songbook 92-93

THE HEARTS OF THE CHILDREN

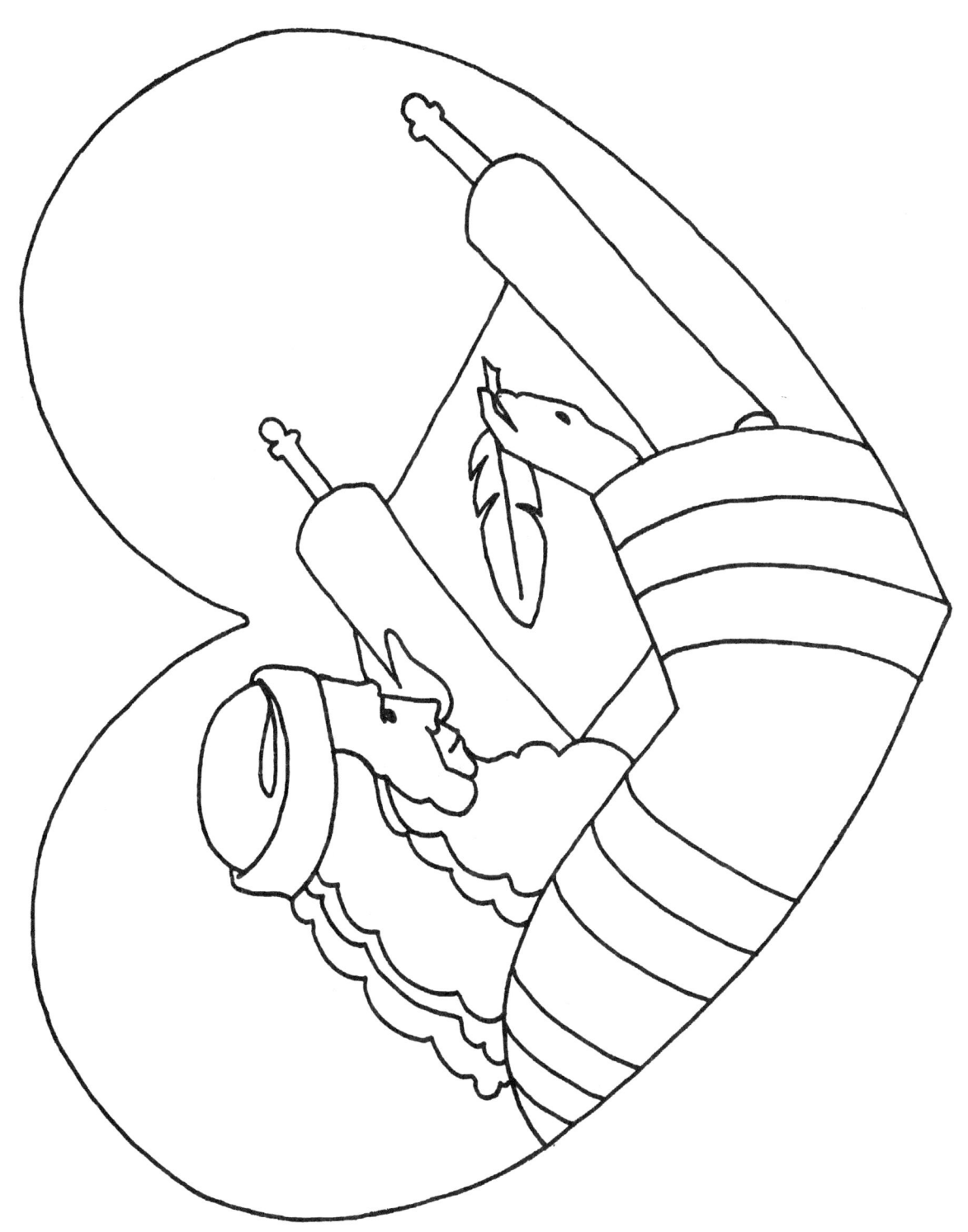

63

THE HEARTS OF THE CHILDREN

Songbook 92-93

Songbook 94

GENEALOGY—I AM DOING IT

GENEALOGY—I AM DOING IT

Songbook 94

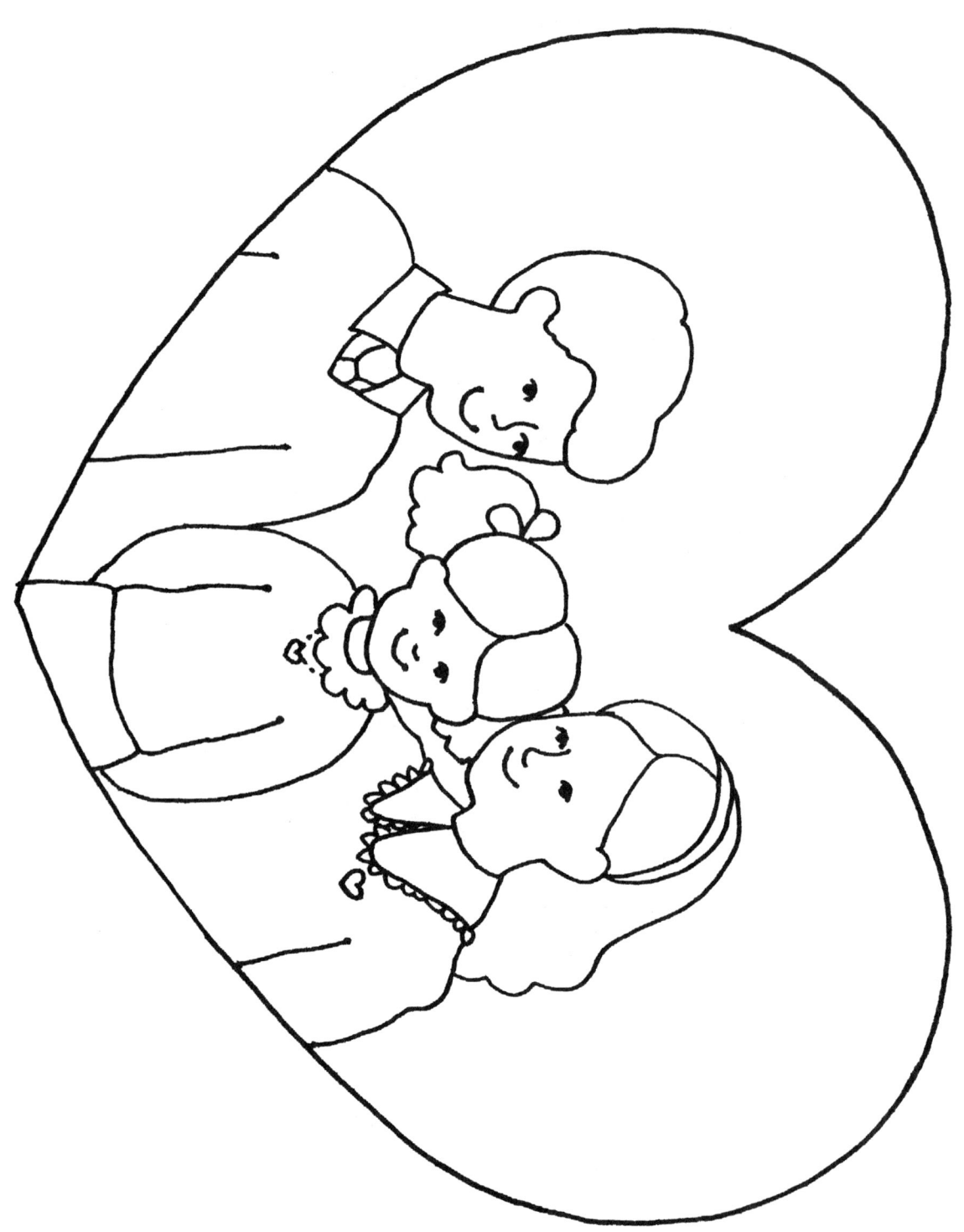

Songbook 95

I LOVE TO SEE THE TEMPLE

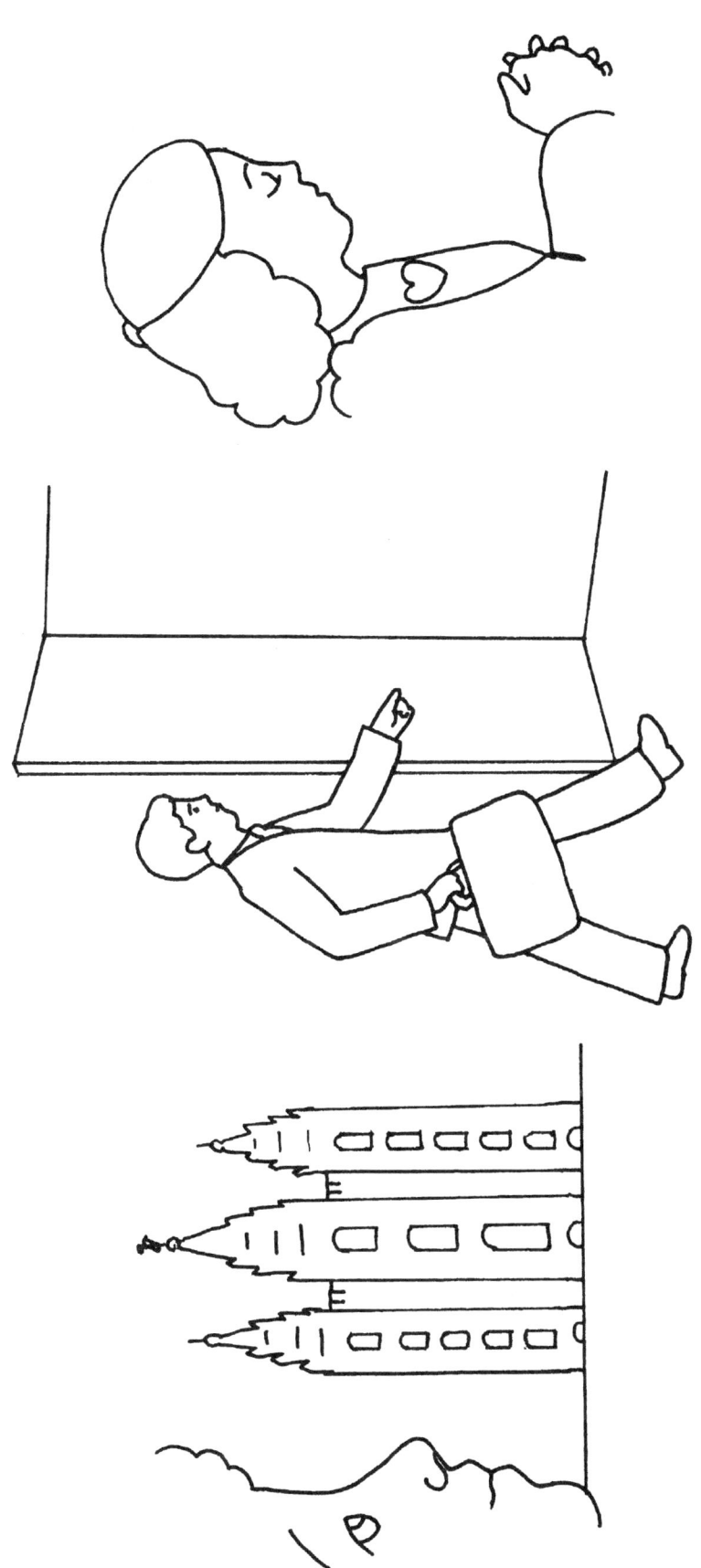

I LOVE TO SEE THE TEMPLE

Songbook 95

Songbook
96-97

FAITH

FAITH

Songbook 96-97

Songbook
98

REPENTANCE

BAPTISM

Songbook
100-1

72

Songbook 103

WHEN I AM BAPTIZED

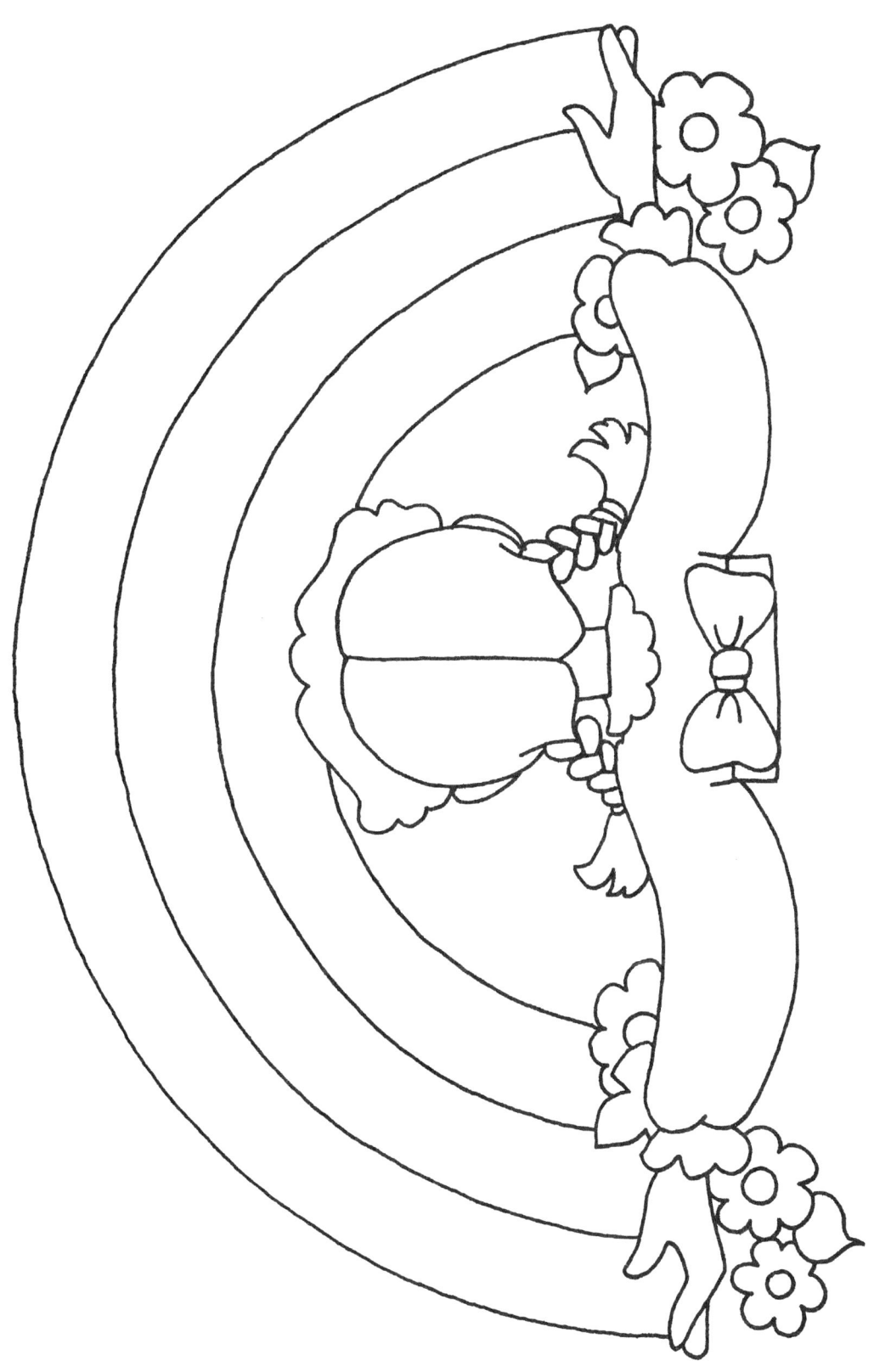

73

I LIKE MY BIRTHDAYS

Songbook 104

Songbook 107

LISTEN, LISTEN

SEEK THE LORD EARLY

Songbook 108

Songbook 109

SEARCH, PONDER AND PRAY

FOLLOW THE PROPHET

Songbook 110-11

78

Songbook 109

SEARCH, PONDER AND PRAY

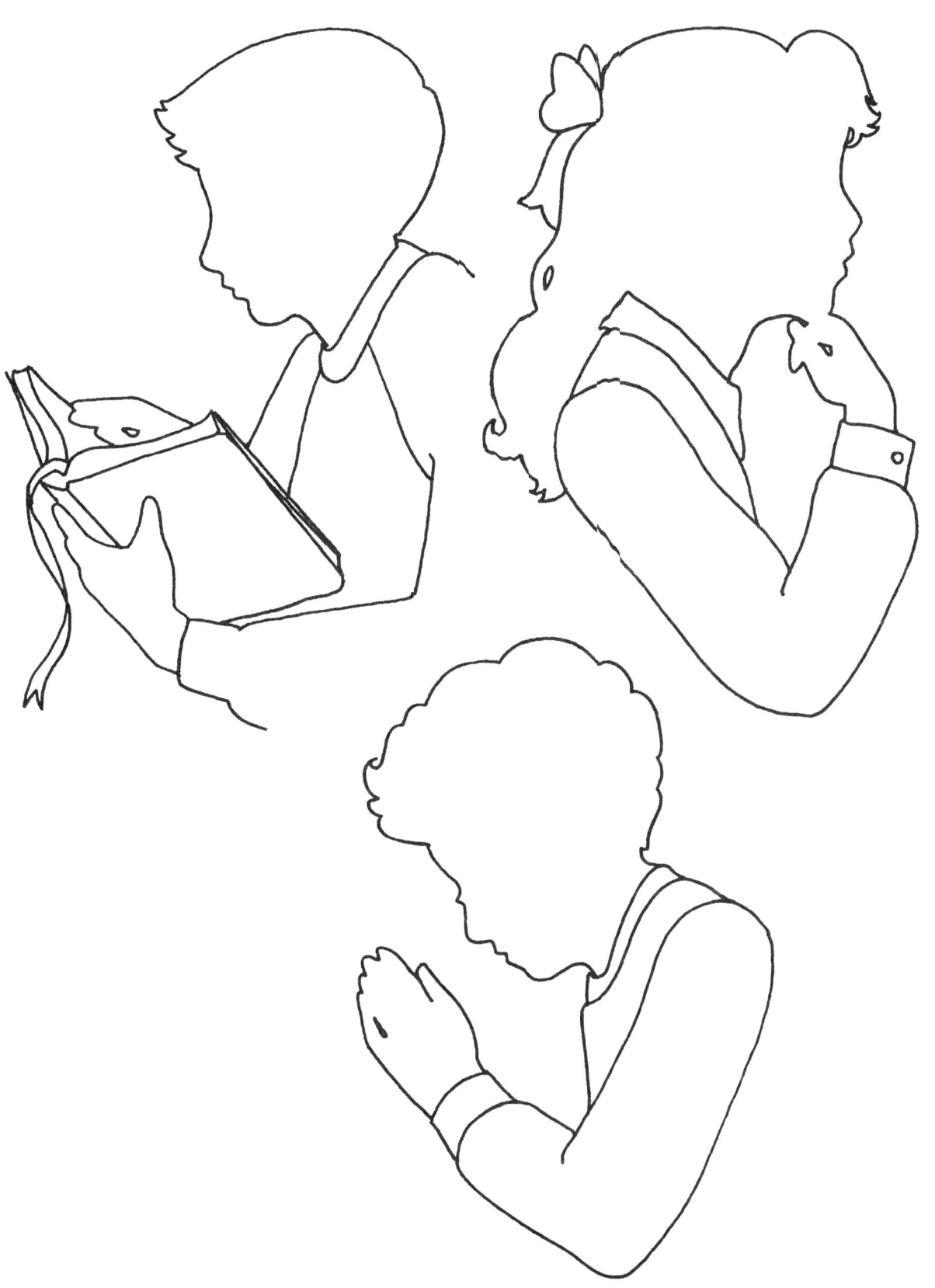

FOLLOW THE PROPHET

Songbook
110-11

78

Songbook
110-11

FOLLOW THE PROPHET

79

BOOK OF MORMON STORIES

Songbook 118-19

Songbook
120-21

NEPHI'S COURAGE

81

THE FIRST ARTICLE OF FAITH

Songbook 122

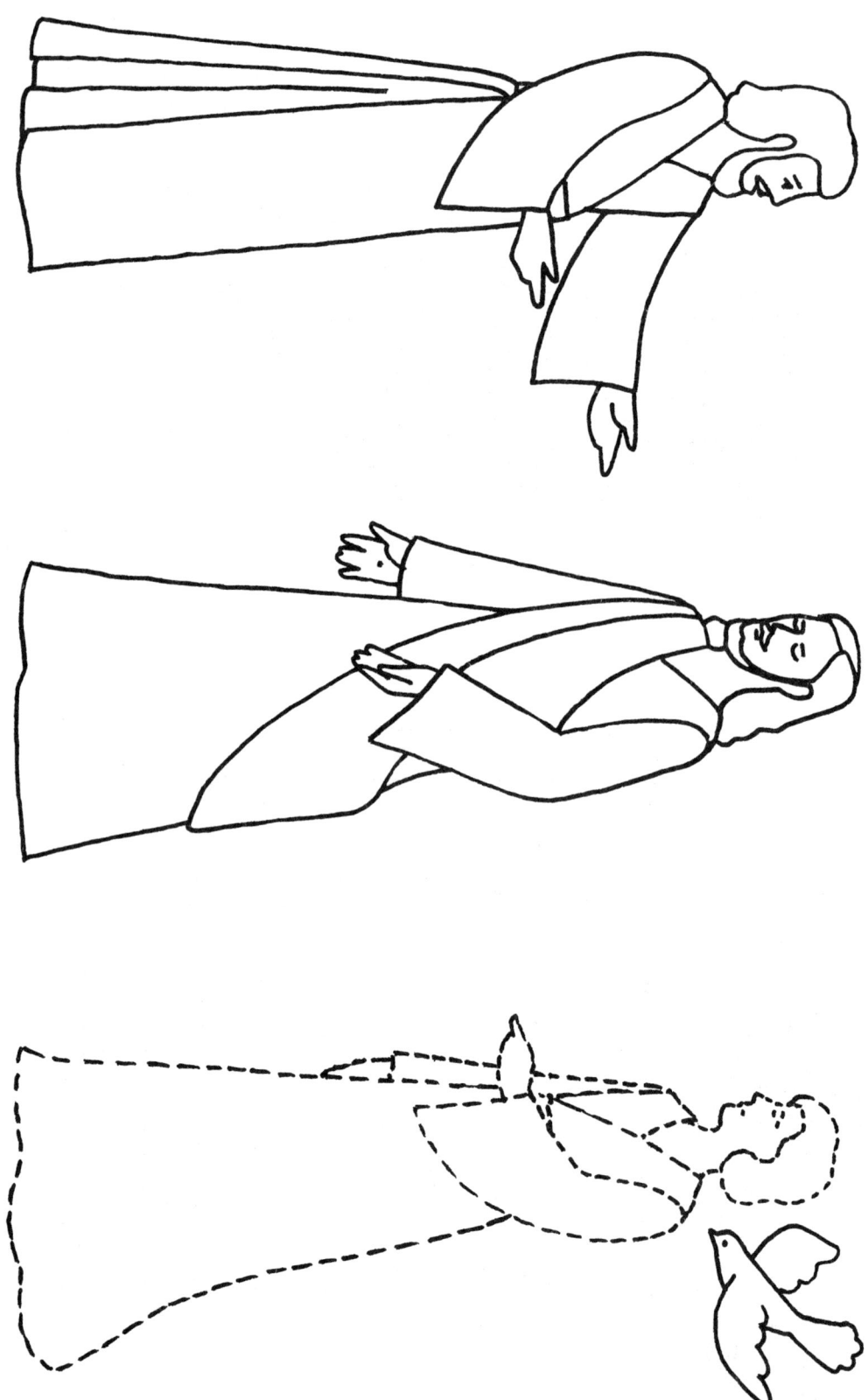

82

Songbook 122

THE SECOND ARTICLE OF FAITH

83

THE THIRD ARTICLE OF FAITH

Songbook 123

Songbook 124

THE FOURTH ARTICLE OF FAITH

THE FIFTH ARTICLE OF FAITH

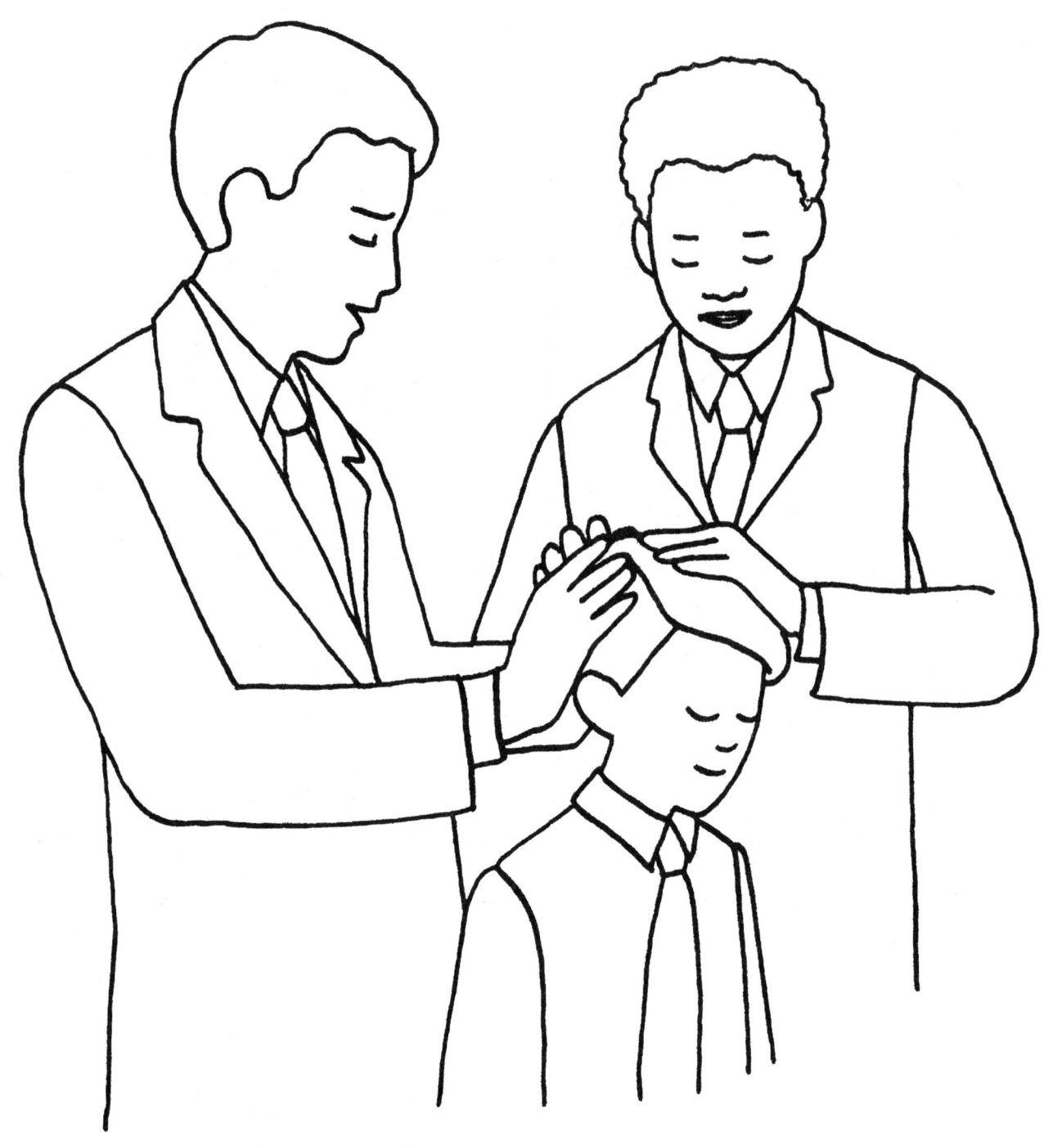

THE SIXTH ARTICLE OF FAITH

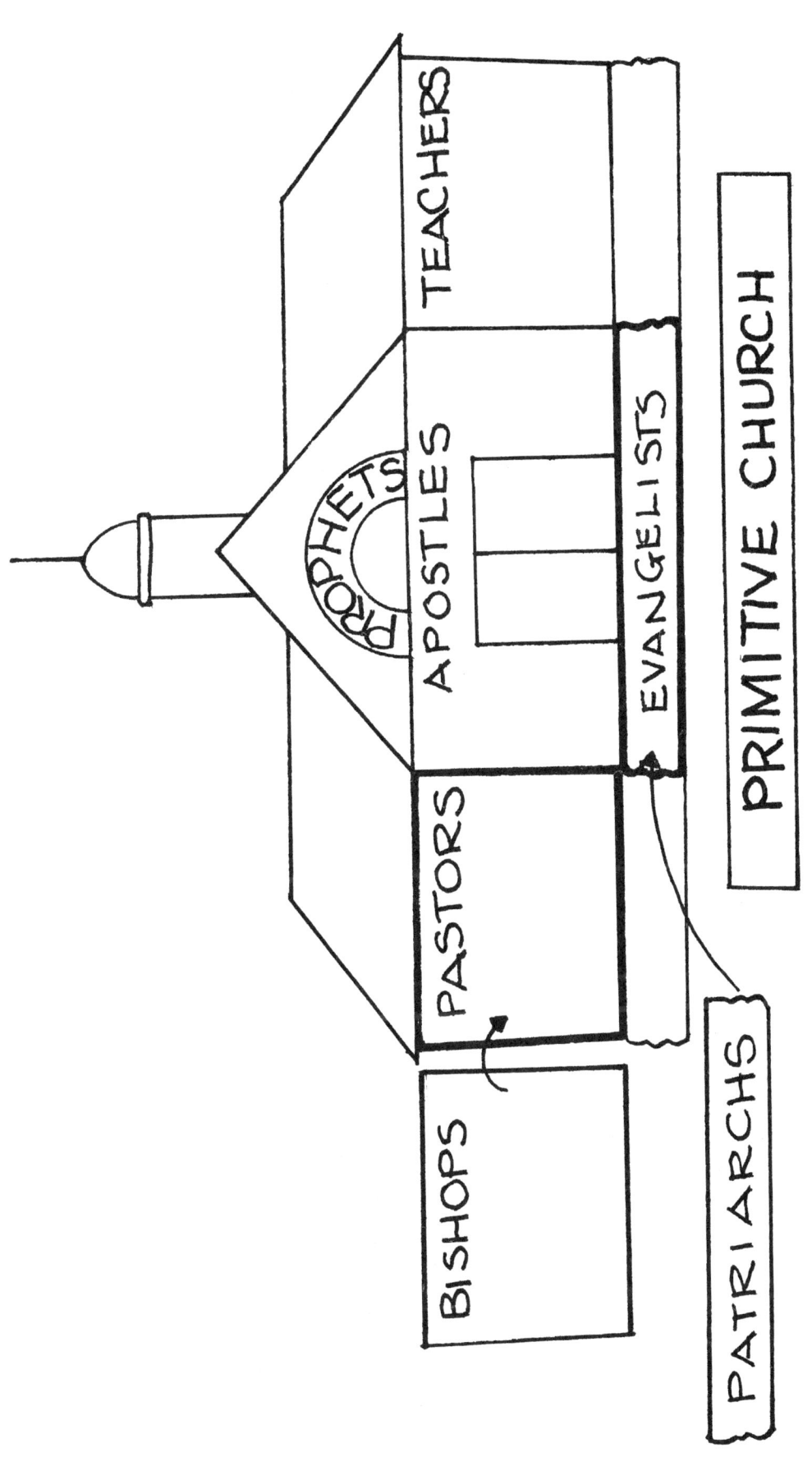

THE SEVENTH ARTICLE OF FAITH

Songbook 126

GIFT OF TONGUES

INTERPRETATION OF TONGUES

THE EIGHTH ARTICLE OF FAITH

Songbook 127

THE ELEVENTH ARTICLE OF FAITH

Songbook 130

90

THE TWELFTH ARTICLE OF FAITH

LATTER-DAY PROPHETS

Songbook 134

Songbook
135

OUR BISHOP

93

LOVE ONE ANOTHER

Songbook
136-37

94

Songbook 138-39

WHERE LOVE IS

95

I'LL WALK WITH YOU

Songbook 140-1

96

Songbook 140-1

I'LL WALK WITH YOU

97

I'LL WALK WITH YOU

Songbook 140-1

Songbook 145

KINDNESS BEGINS WITH ME

HUM YOUR FAVORITE HYMN

Songbook 152

100

Songbook 153

THE LORD GAVE ME A TEMPLE

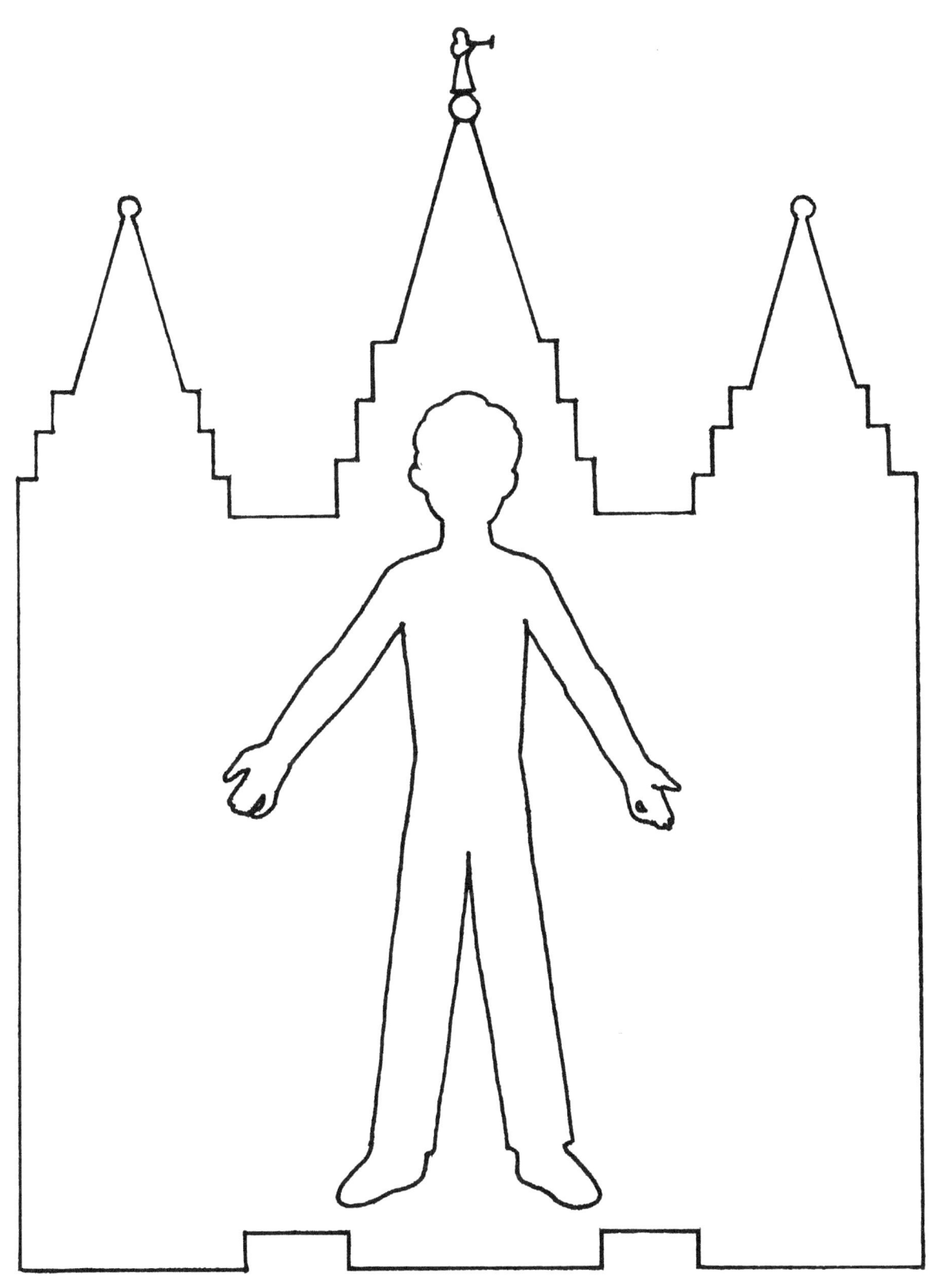

101

THE WORD OF WISDOM

Songbook
154-55

102

Songbook 155

REMEMBER THE SABBATH DAY

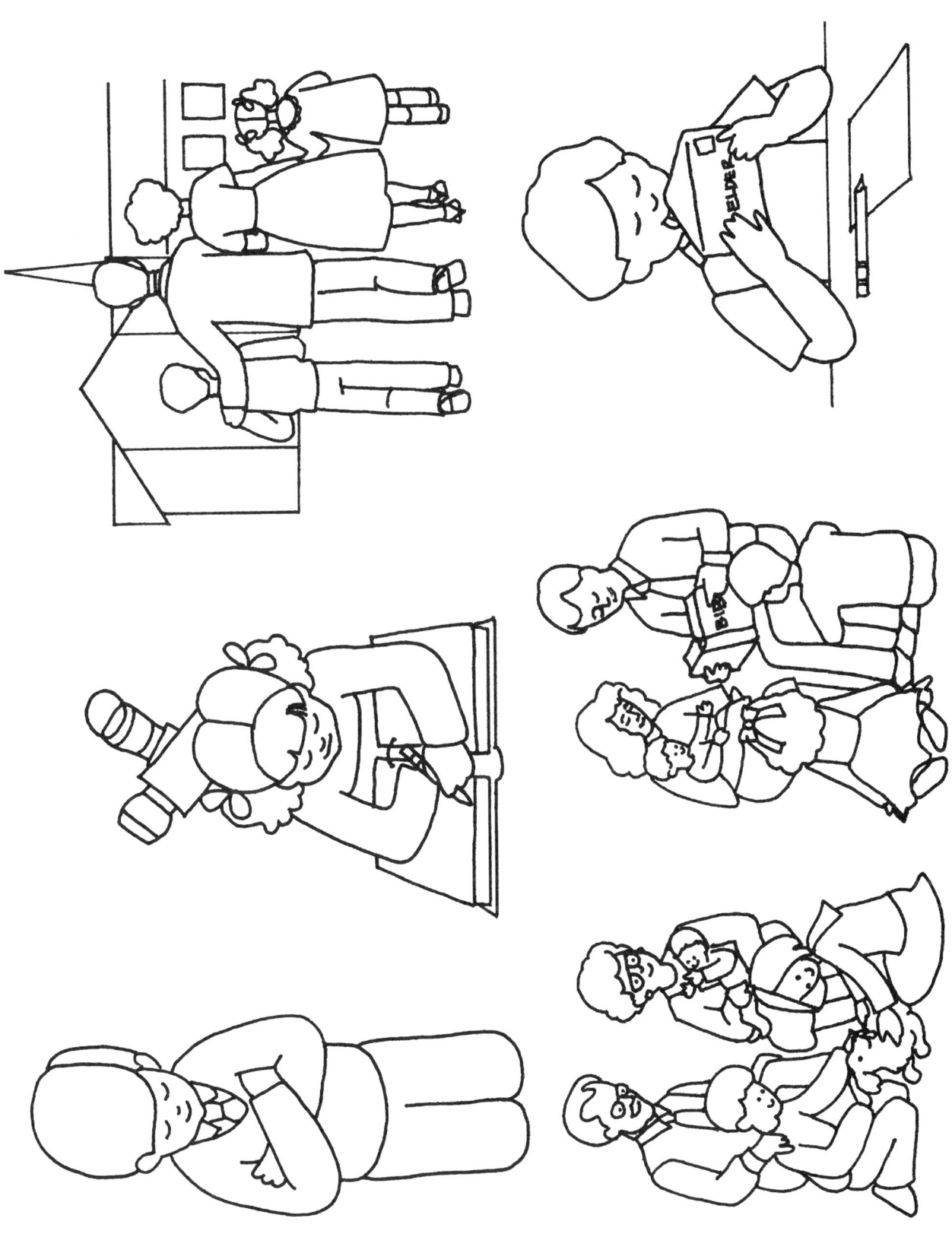

103

THE CHAPEL DOORS

Songbook 156

104

DARE TO DO RIGHT

I PLEDGE MYSELF TO LOVE THE RIGHT

Songbook 161

106

Songbook 163

I AM LIKE A STAR

107

GO THE SECOND MILE

Songbook 167

Songbook 168

I WANT TO BE A MISSIONARY NOW

I HOPE THEY CALL ME ON A MISSION

Songbook 169

110

Songbook
174-75

CALLED TO SERVE

111

TEACHER, DO YOU LOVE ME?

Songbook 178-79

112

Songbook 180-81

HOW DEAR TO GOD ARE LITTLE CHILDREN

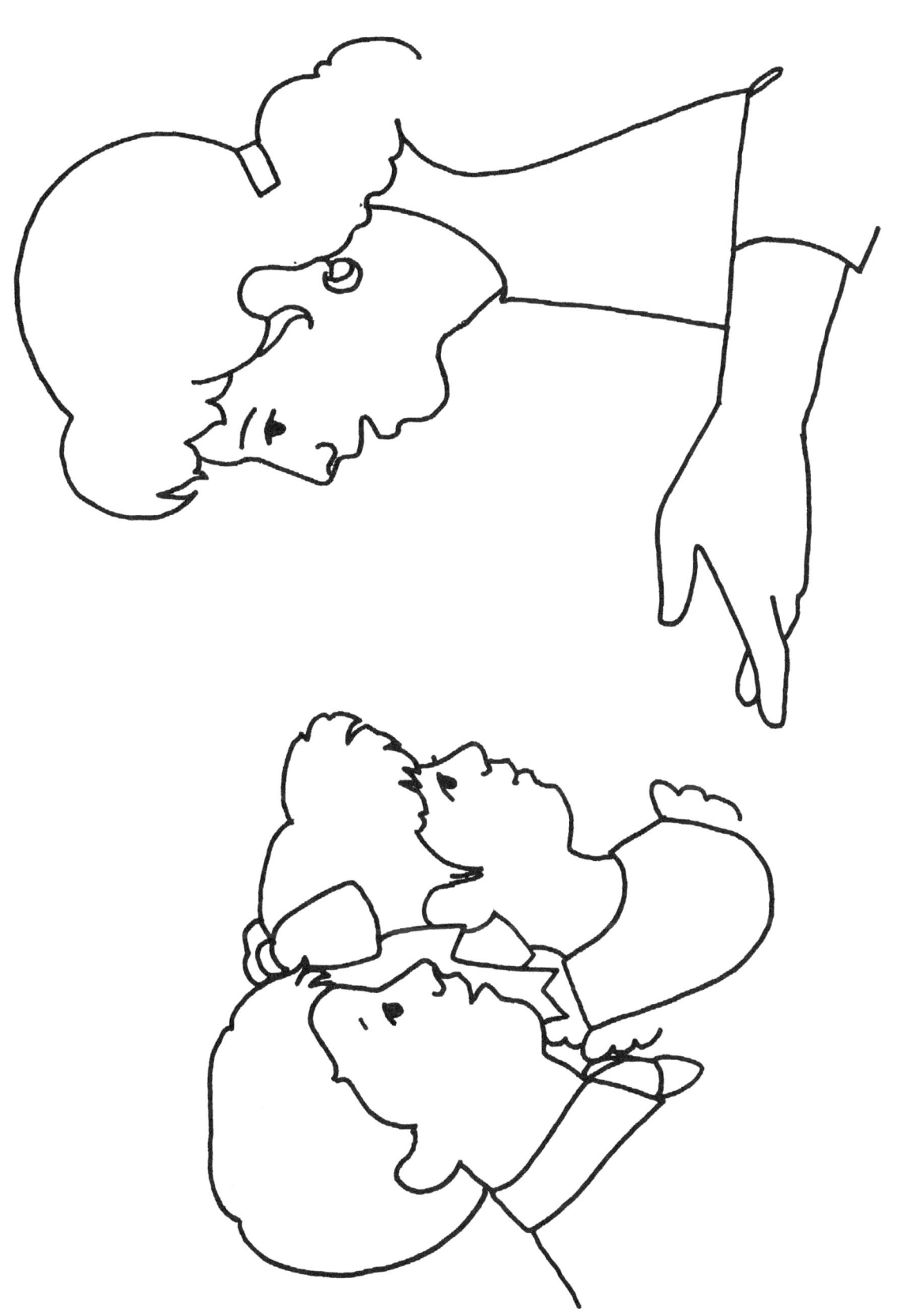

113

HOW WILL THEY KNOW?

Songbook
182-83

114

Songbook 188

FAMILIES CAN BE TOGETHER FOREVER

HOME

Songbook 192

Songbook 194

THE FAMILY

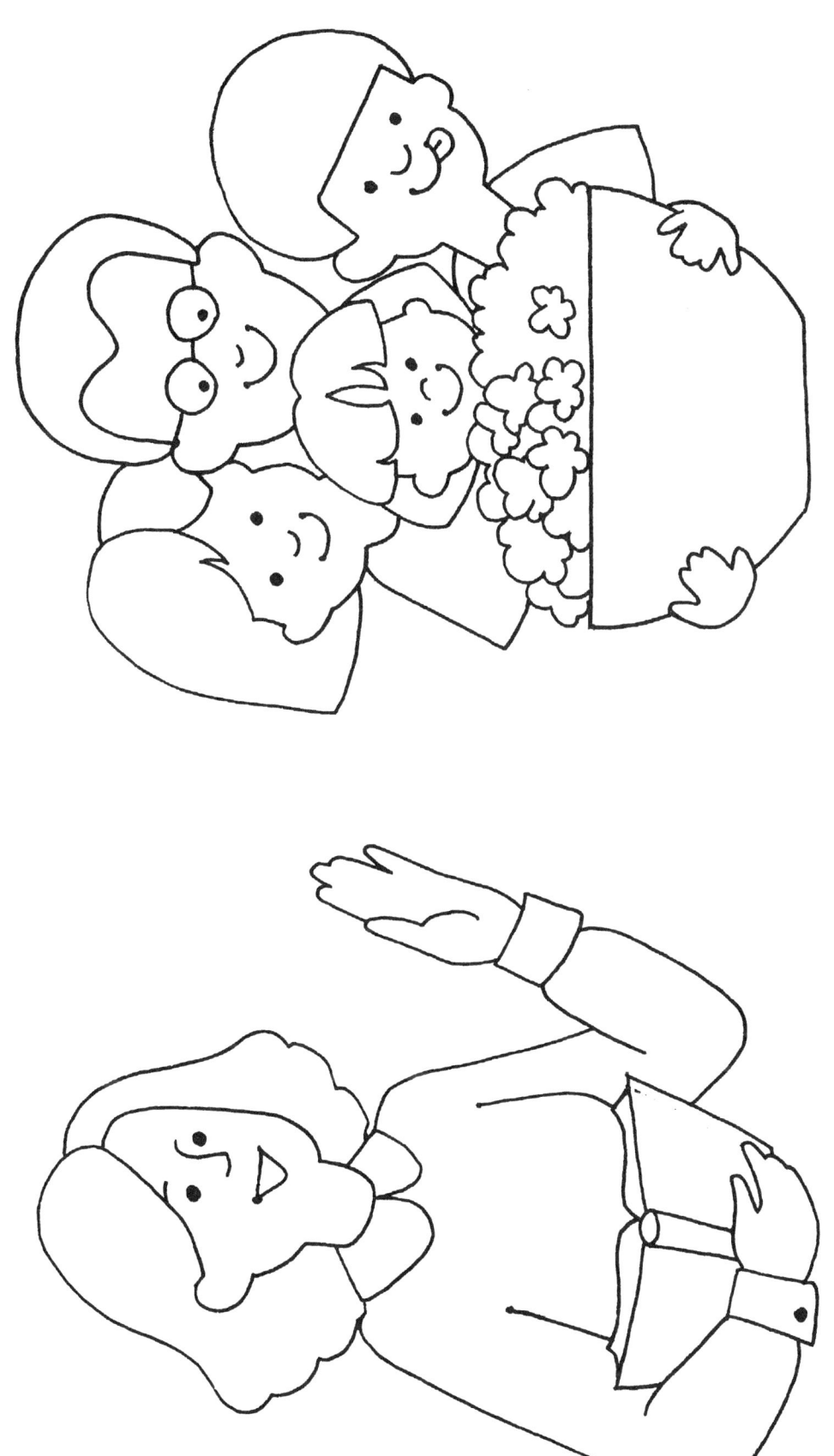

117

FAMILY NIGHT

Songbook 195

Songbook 197

A HAPPY HELPER

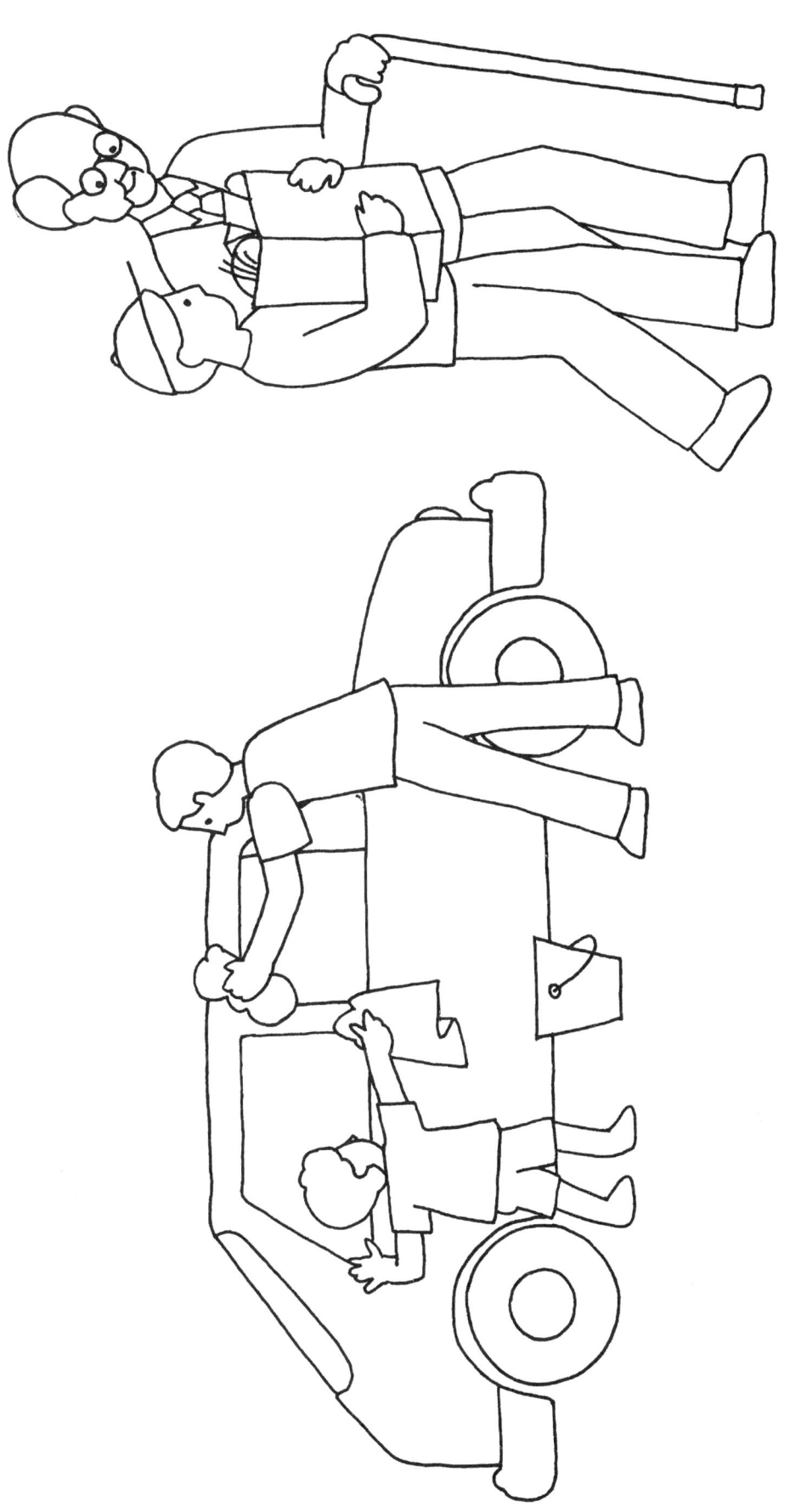

QUICKLY I'LL OBEY

Songbook 197

Songbook 197

QUICKLY I'LL OBEY

121

A HAPPY FAMILY

Songbook 198

122

Songbook 198

WHEN WE'RE HELPING

I HAVE A FAMILY TREE

Songbook 199

124

Songbook 200

GRANDMOTHER

WHEN GRANDPA COMES

Songbook 201

Songbook 202

I OFTEN GO WALKING

127

MOTHER, TELL ME THE STORY

Songbook
204-5

128

Songbook 208

THE DEAREST NAMES

FATHERS

Songbook
209

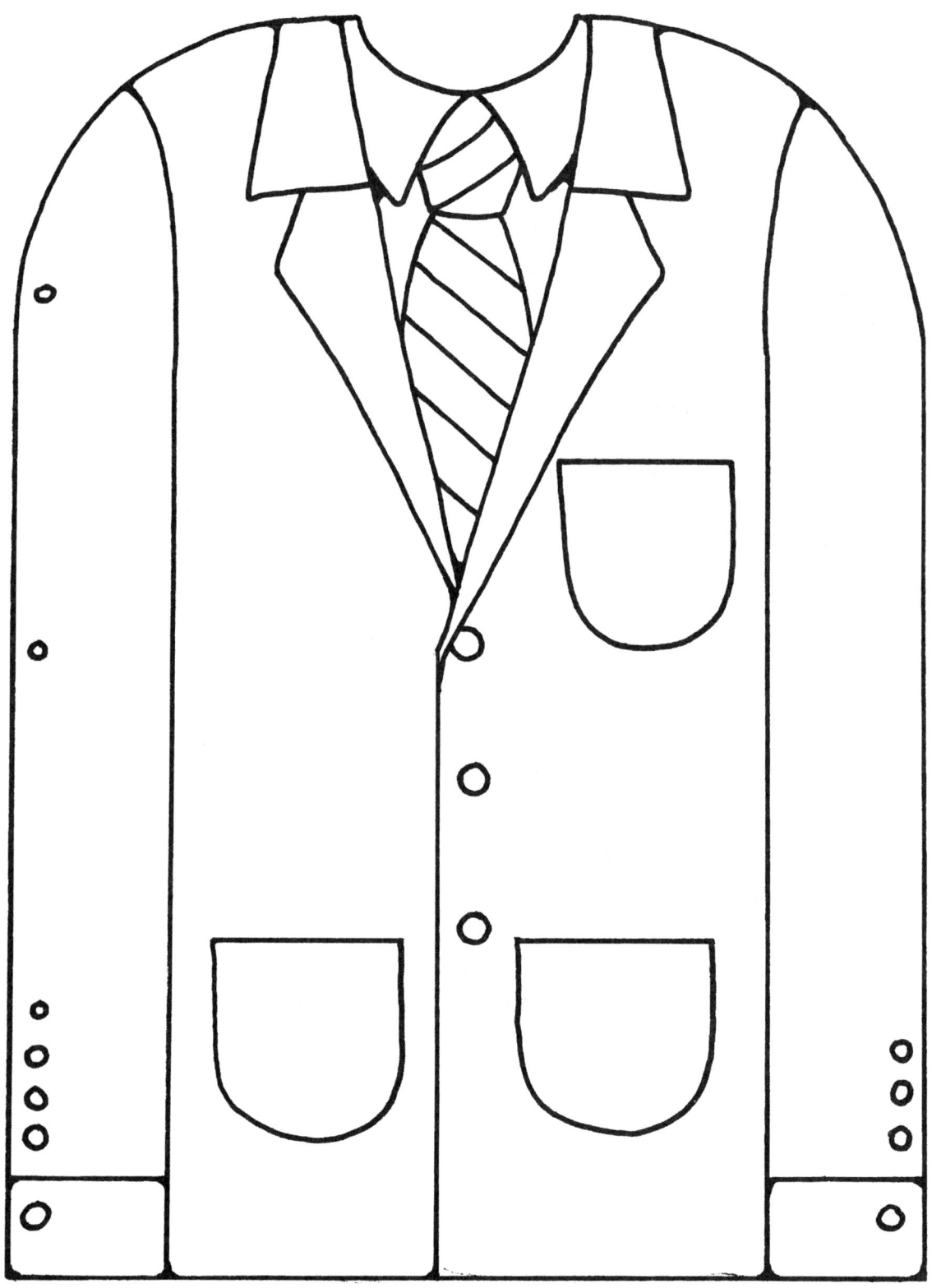

130

DADDY'S HOMECOMING

Songbook 210

Songbook 214 — PIONEER CHILDREN SANG AS THEY WALKED

133

PIONEER CHILDREN WERE QUICK TO OBEY

Songbook 215

Songbook 216-17

LITTLE PIONEER CHILDREN

135

WESTWARD HO!

Songbook 217

136

Songbook 217

WESTWARD HO!

TO BE A PIONEER

Songbook 218-19

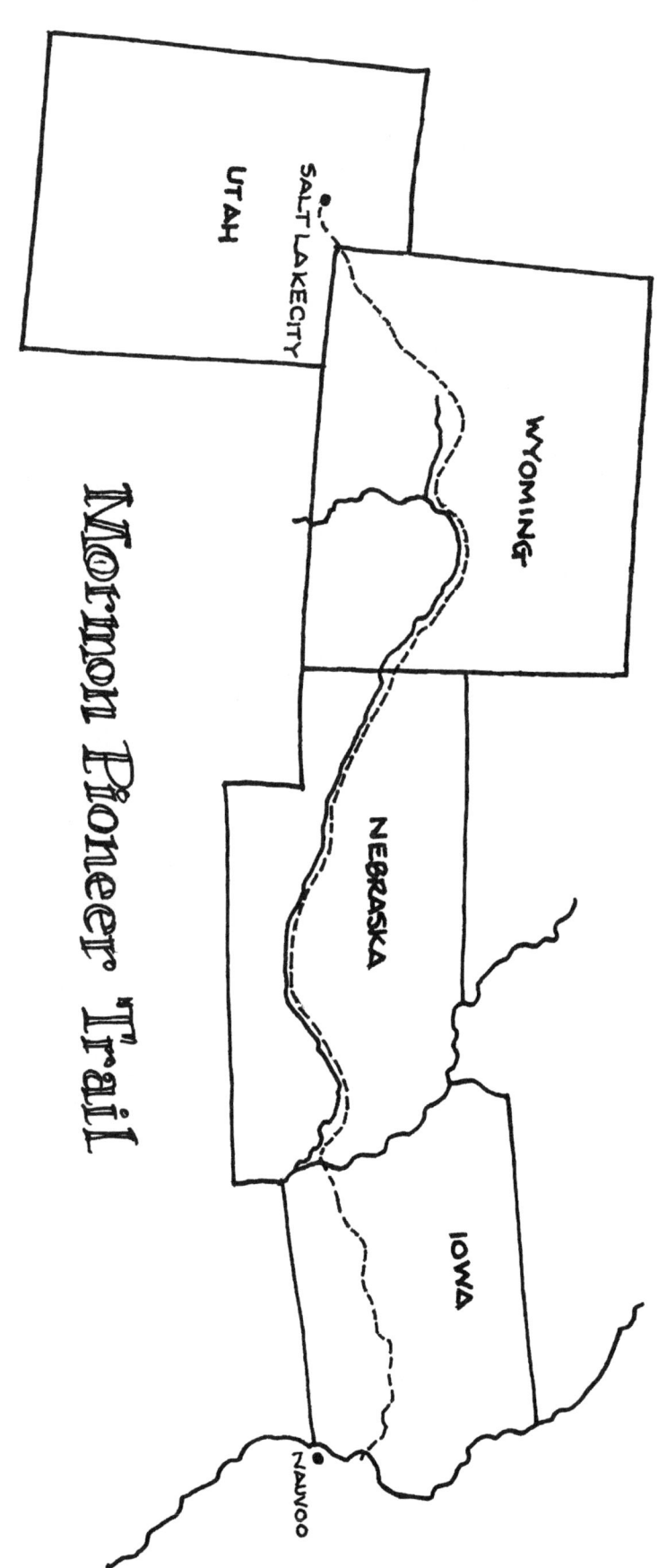

138

Songbook
219

THE OXCART

THE HANDCART SONG

Songbook 220

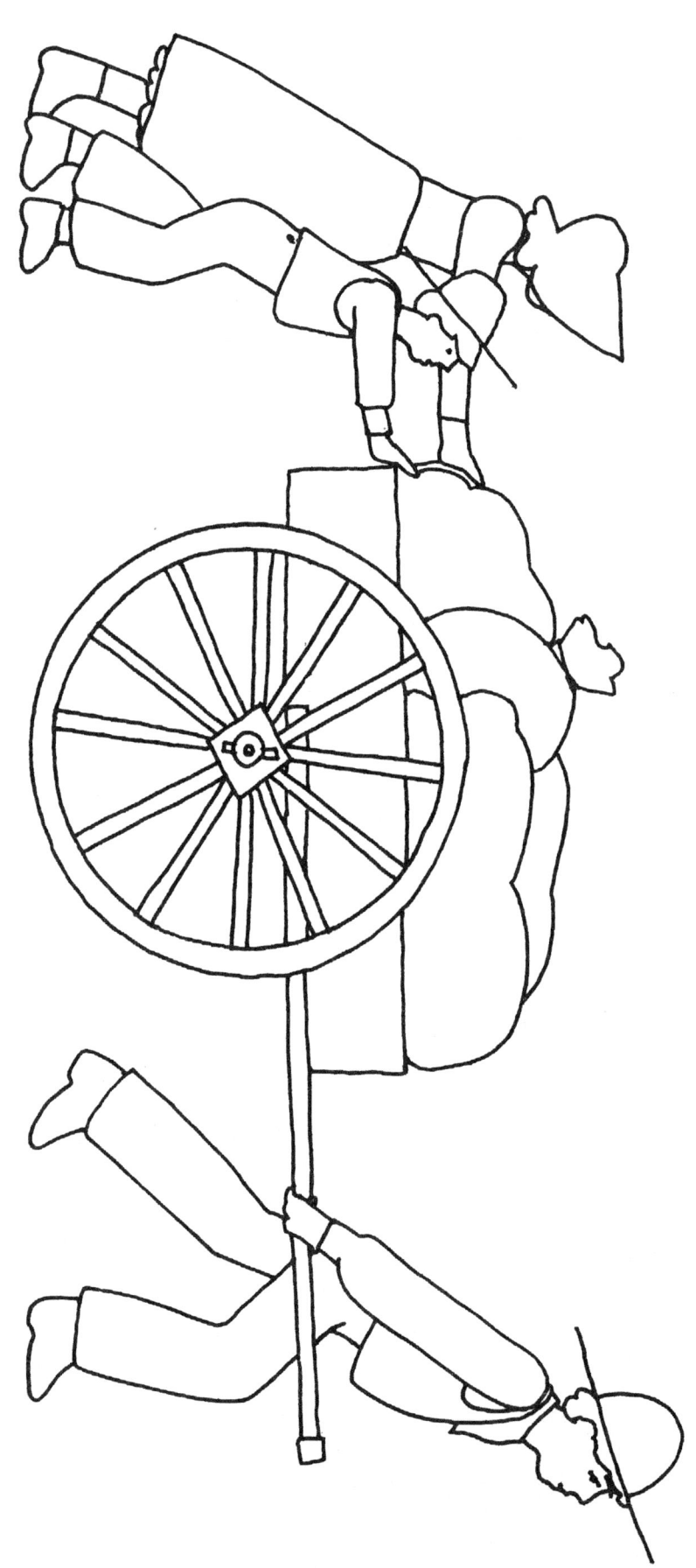

Songbook 221

COVERED WAGONS

GOD IS WATCHING OVER ALL

Songbook 229

142

Songbook 229

GOD IS WATCHING OVER ALL

BEAUTY EVERYWHERE

Songbook 232

Songbook 233

THE WORLD IS SO LOVELY

145

BECAUSE GOD LOVES ME

Songbook
234

146

Songbook 237 — THE PROPHET SAID TO PLANT A GARDEN

147

SPRINGTIME IS COMING

Songbook 238

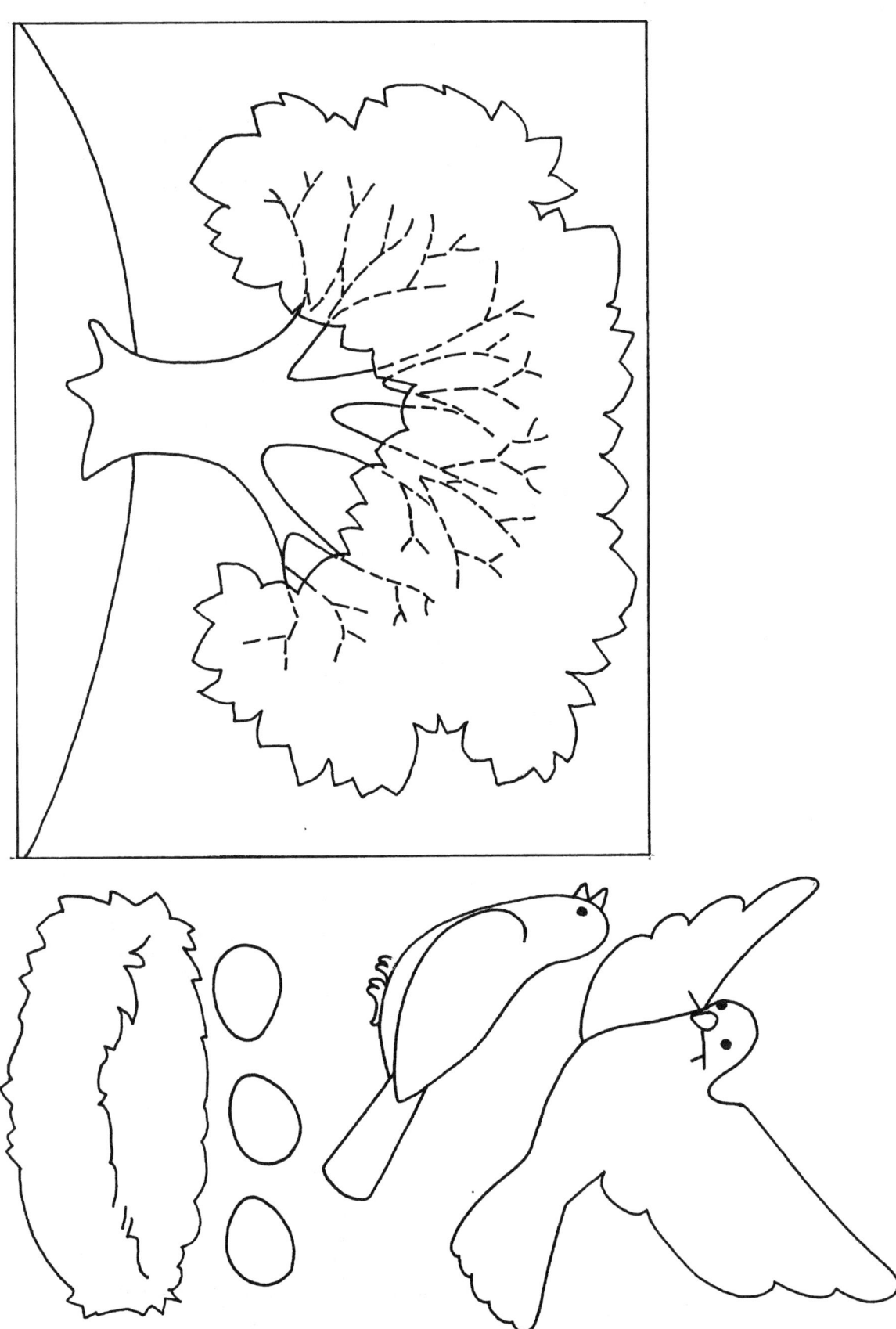

148

Songbook 241

RAIN IS FALLING ALL AROUND

149

LITTLE SEEDS LIE FAST ASLEEP

Songbook 243

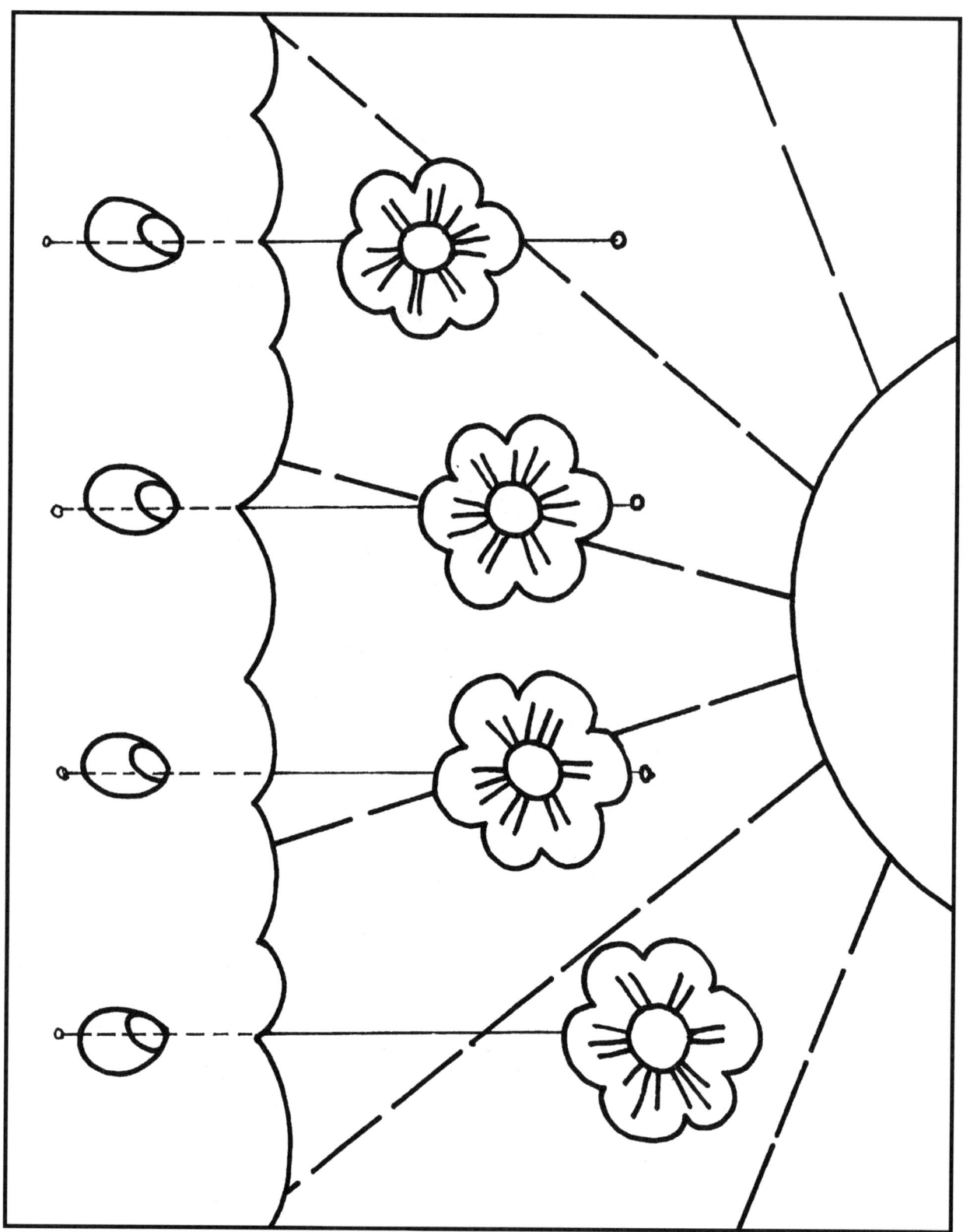

Songbook 245

OH, WHAT DO YOU DO IN THE . . .

AUTUMN DAY

Songbook 247

152

Songbook 248

AUTUMN DAY

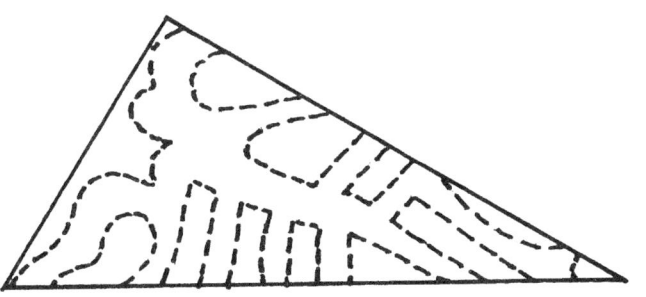

153

SING A SONG

Songbook 253

Songbook 253

FUN TO DO

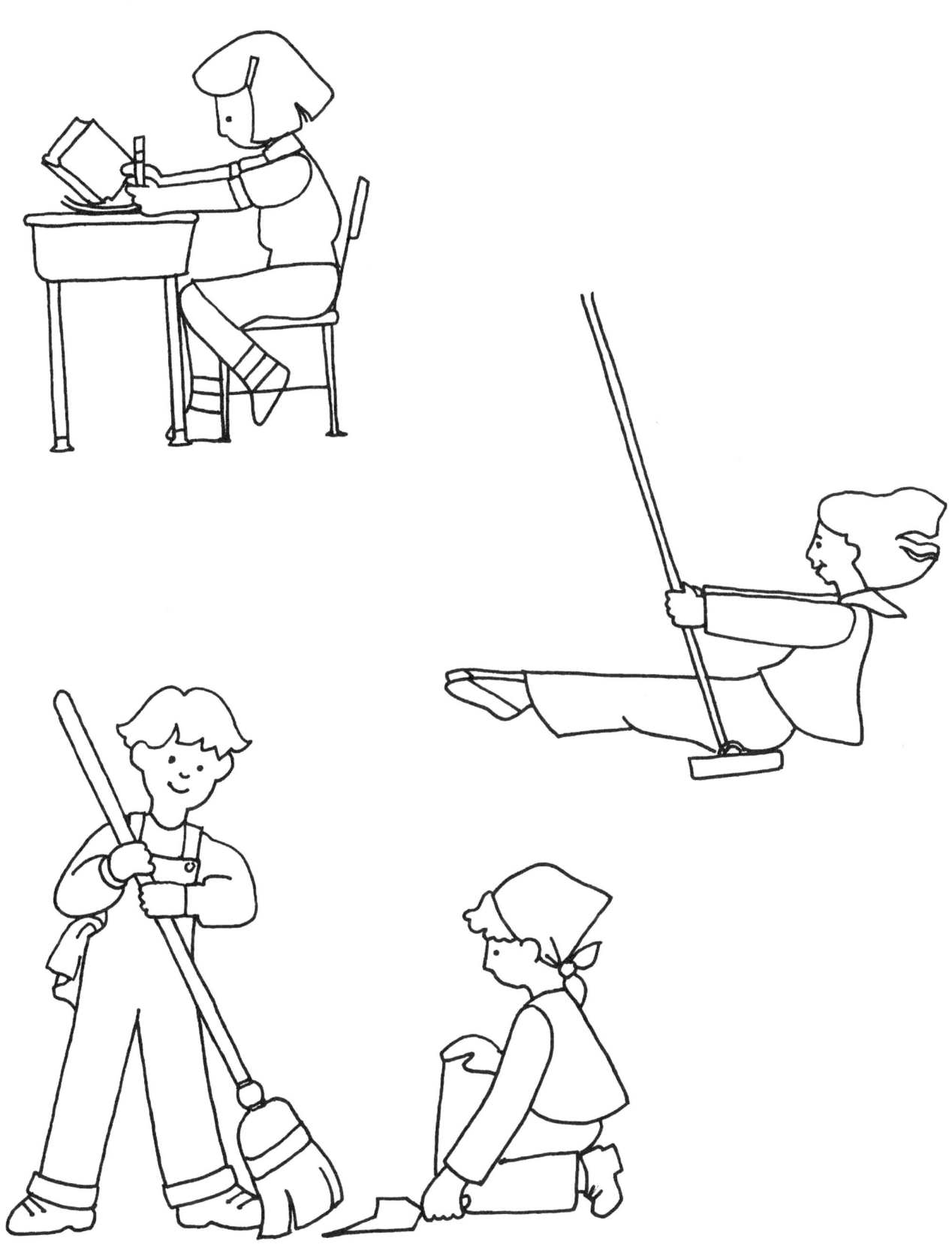

155

OUR DOOR IS ALWAYS OPEN

Songbook
254

Songbook 255

COME WITH ME TO PRIMARY

COME WITH ME TO PRIMARY

Songbook 255

158

Songbook 258

OUR PRIMARY COLORS

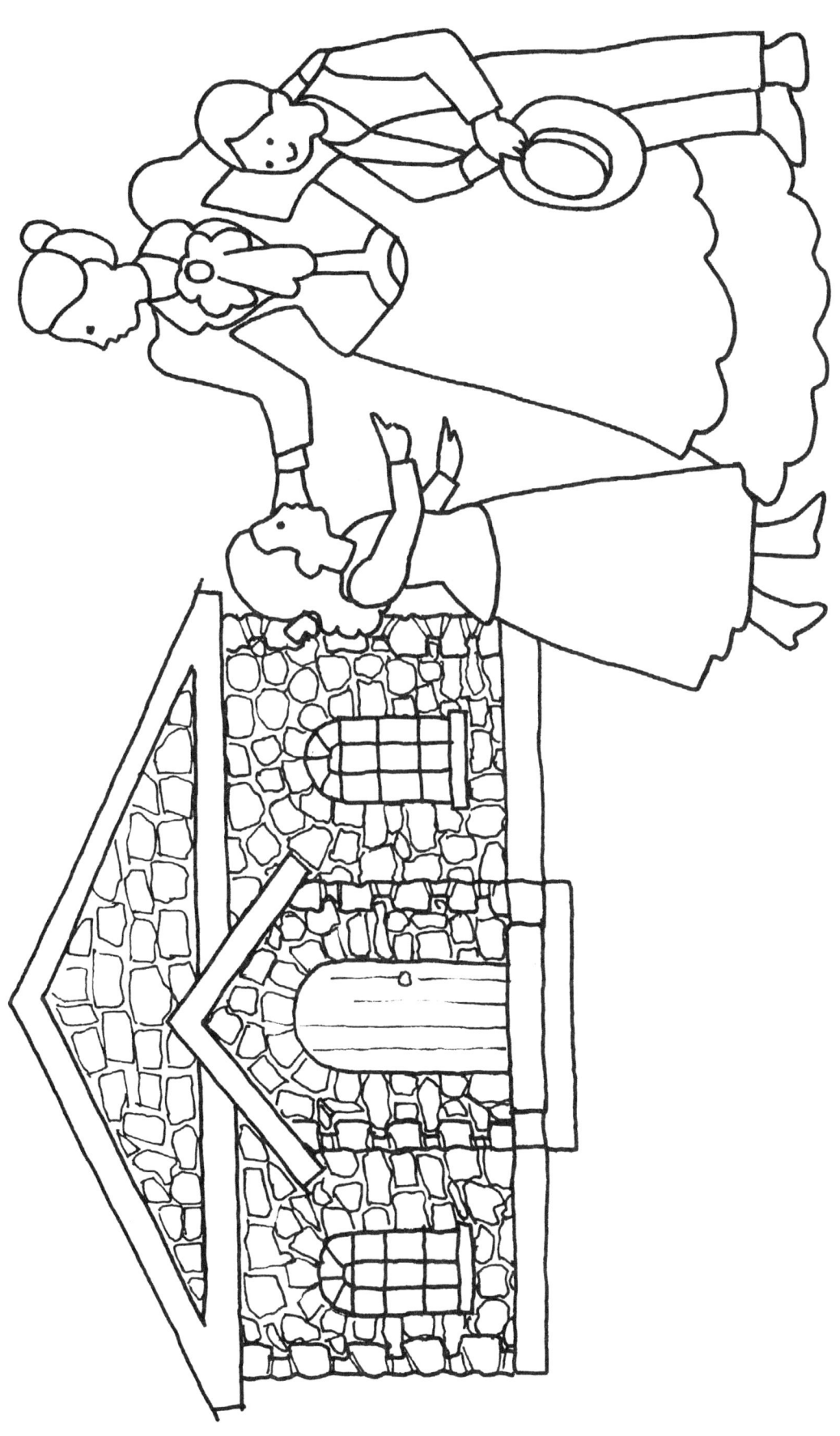

159

FRIENDS ARE FUN

Songbook
262

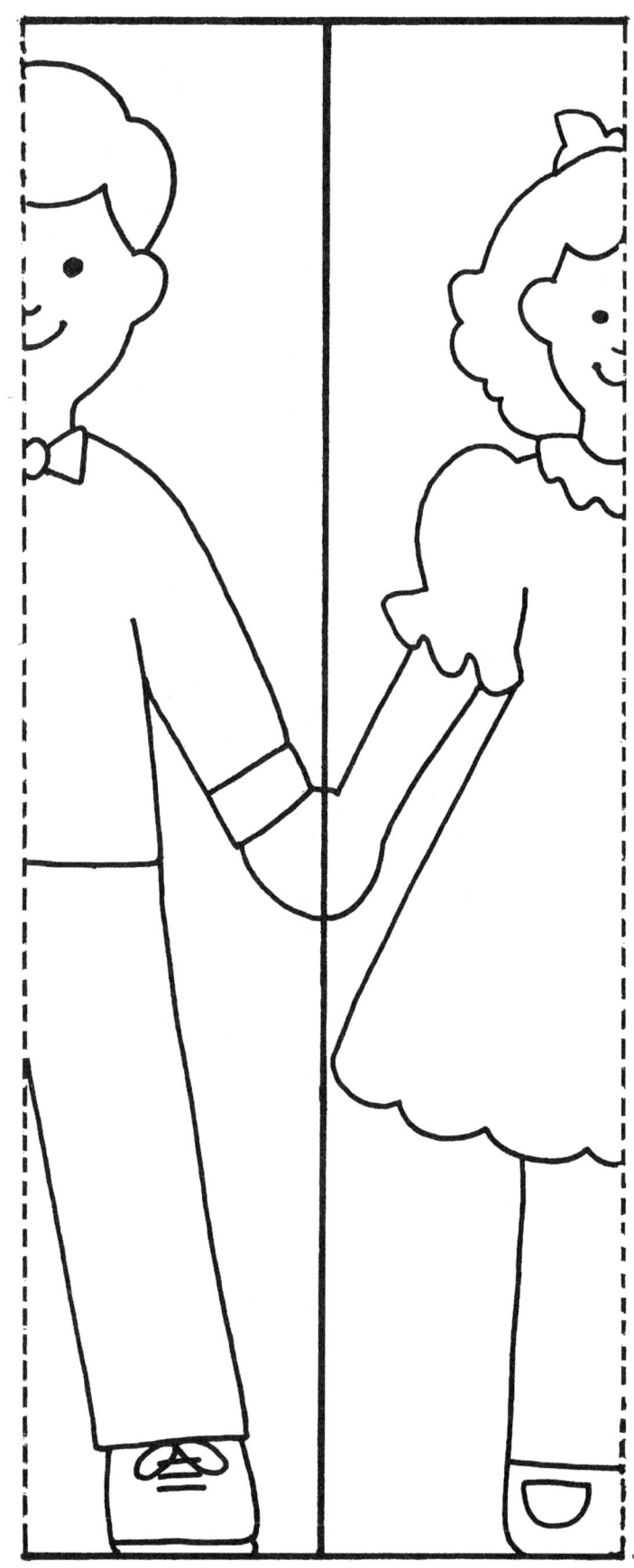

160

Songbook 263

WE ARE DIFFERENT

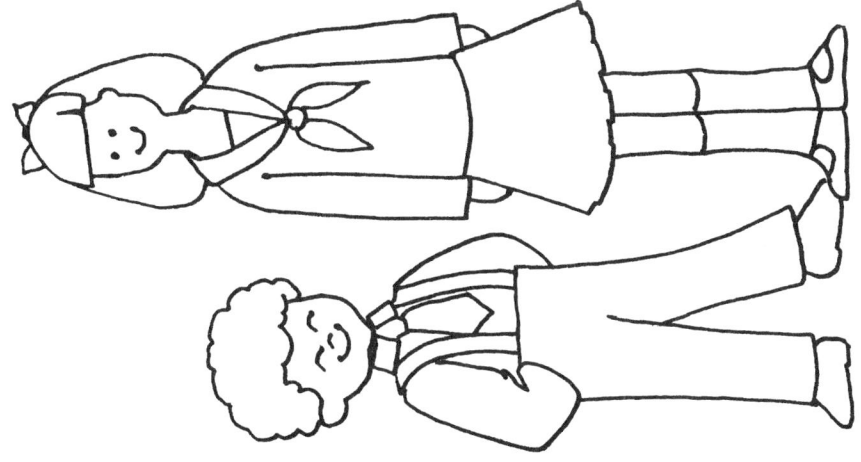

HAPPY SONG

Songbook 264

162

Songbook 266

IF YOU'RE HAPPY

163

SMILES

Songbook
267

164

Songbook 270 — TWO HAPPY FEET

165

TWO HAPPY FEET

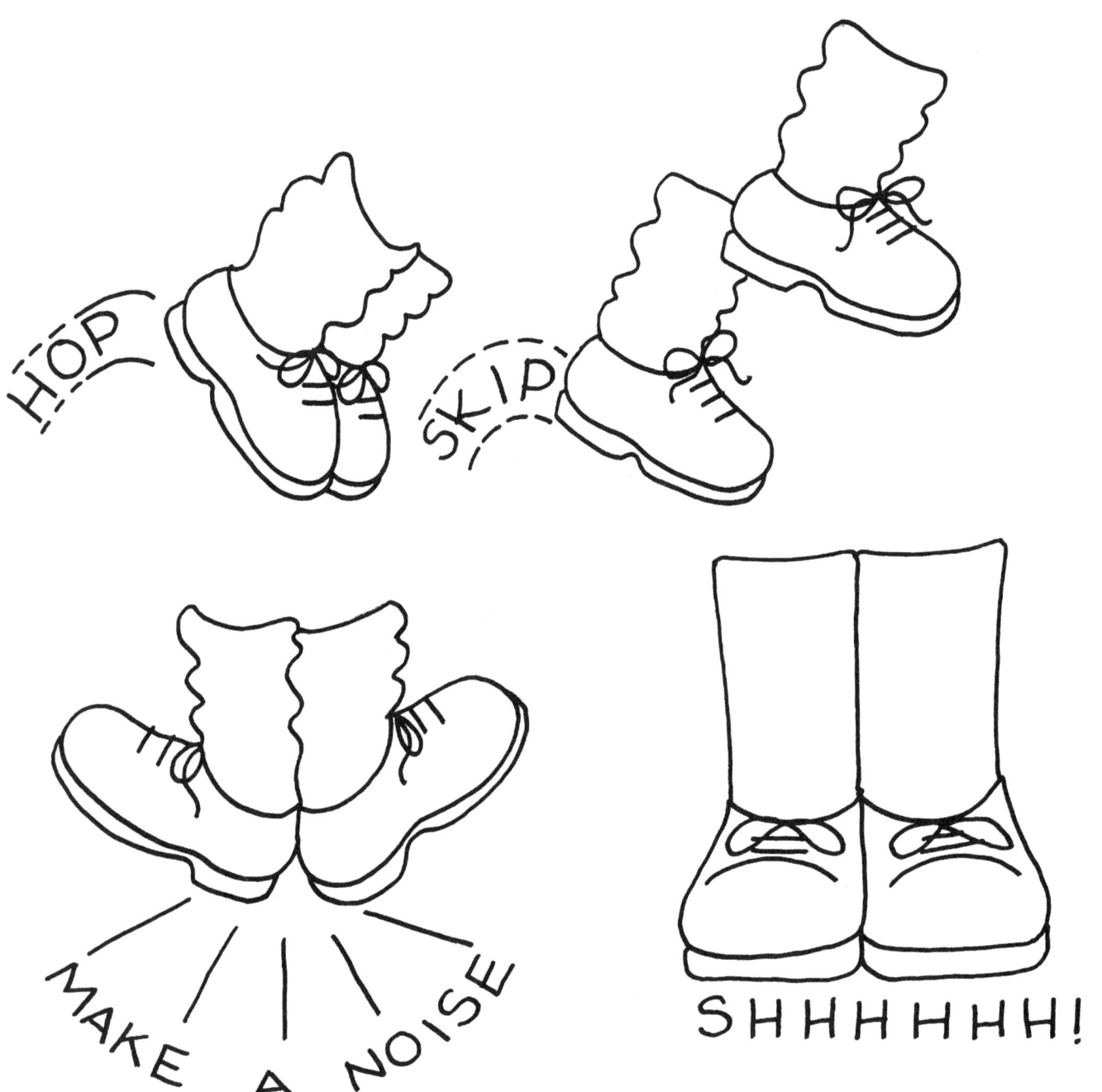

Songbook
277

HINGES

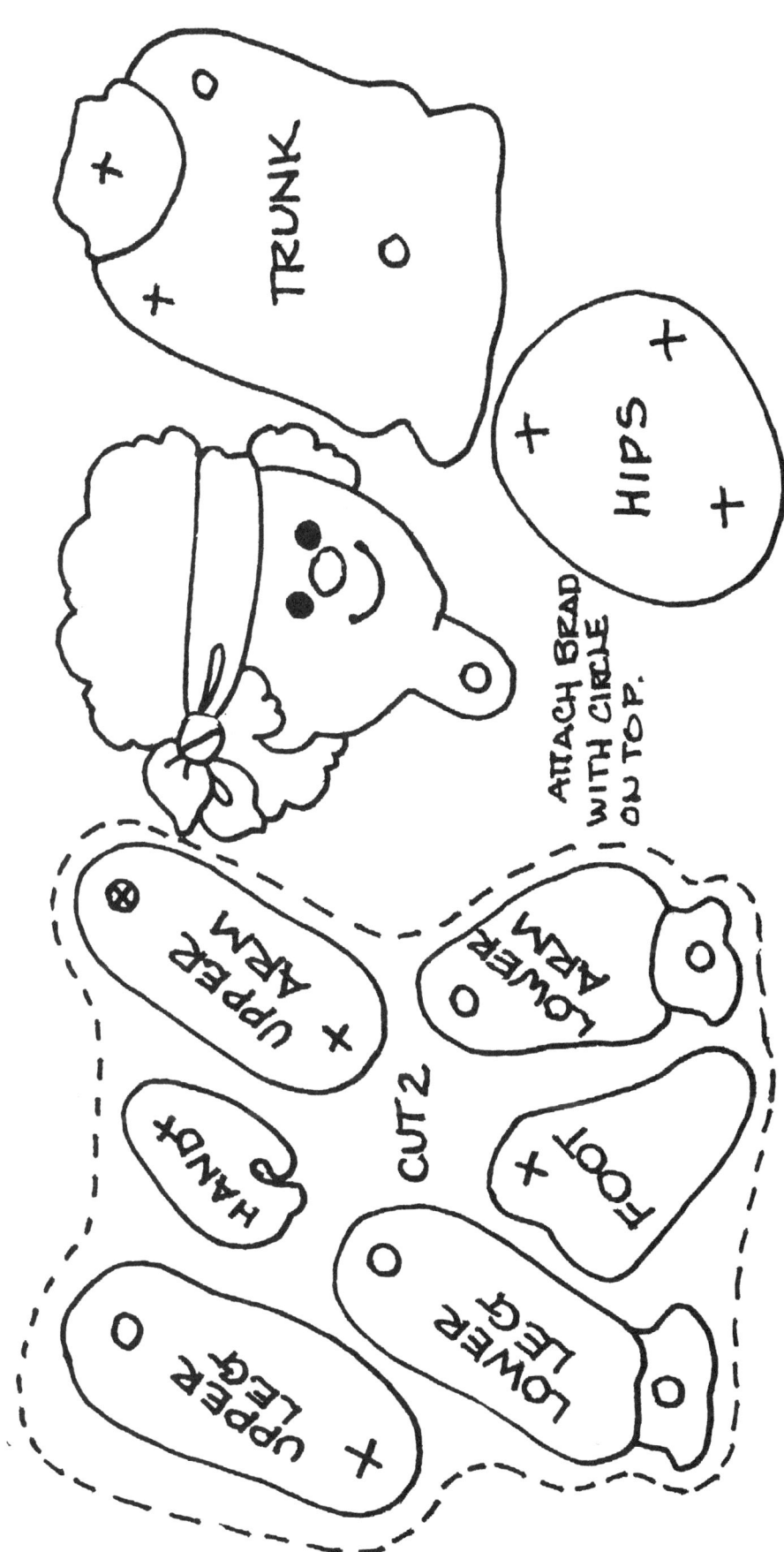

167

HEALTHY, WEALTHY, AND WISE

Songbook 280

Songbook 281

THE WISE MAN AND THE FOOLISH MAN

169

THE WISE MAN AND THE FOOLISH MAN

Songbook 281

FELIZ CUMPLEAÑOS

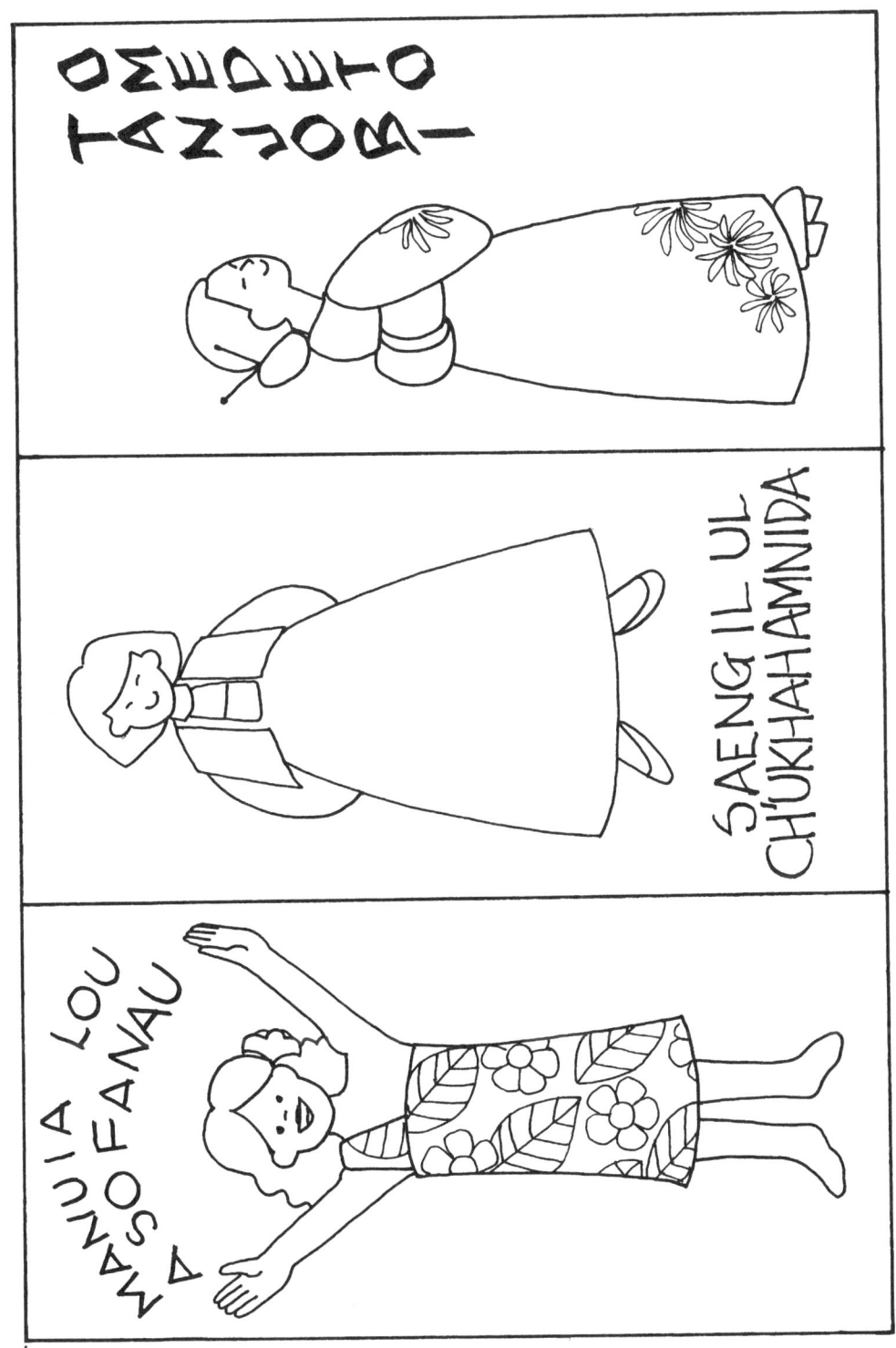

FELIZ CUMPLEAÑOS

Songbook
284

HAPPY, HAPPY BIRTHDAY

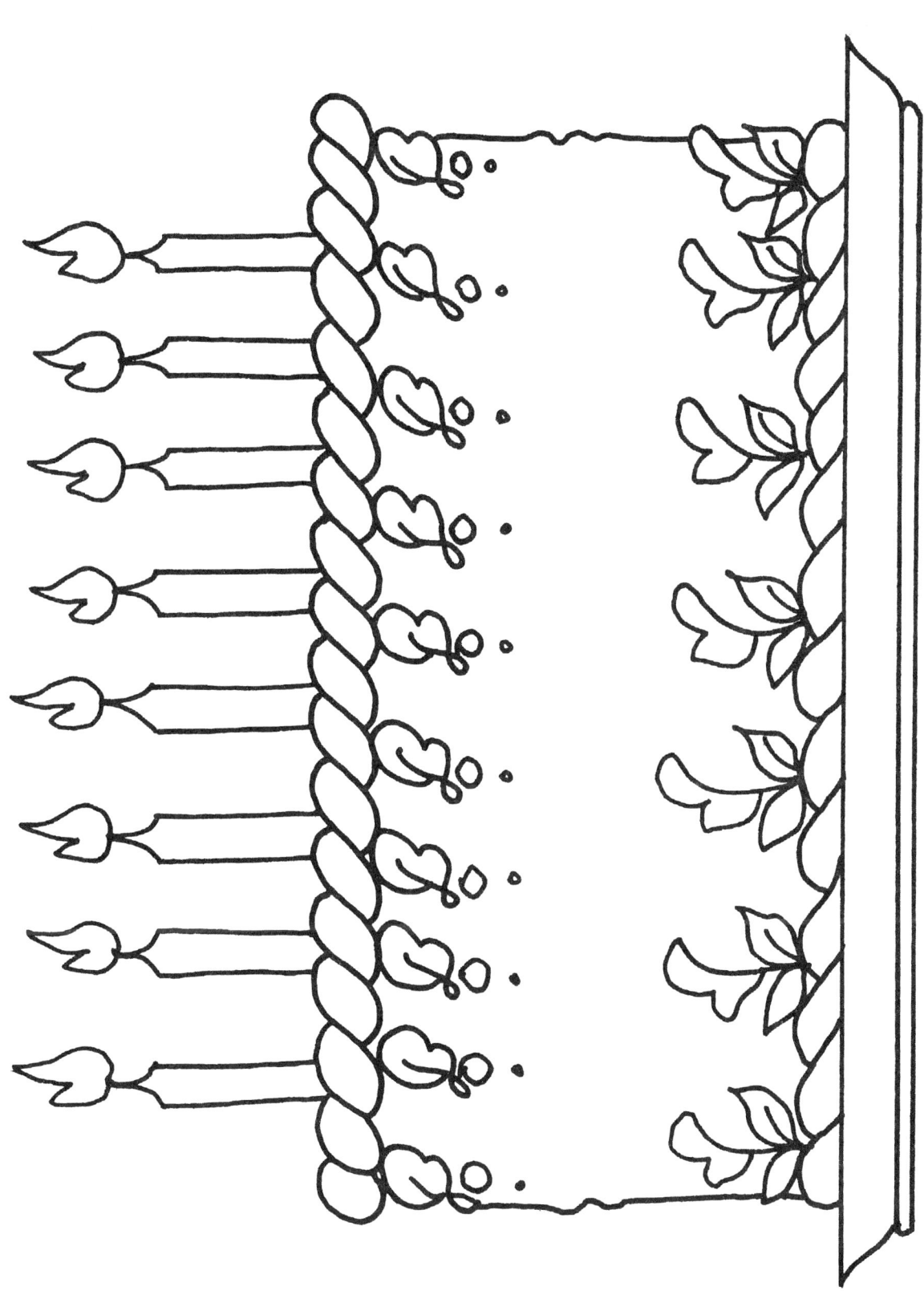

173

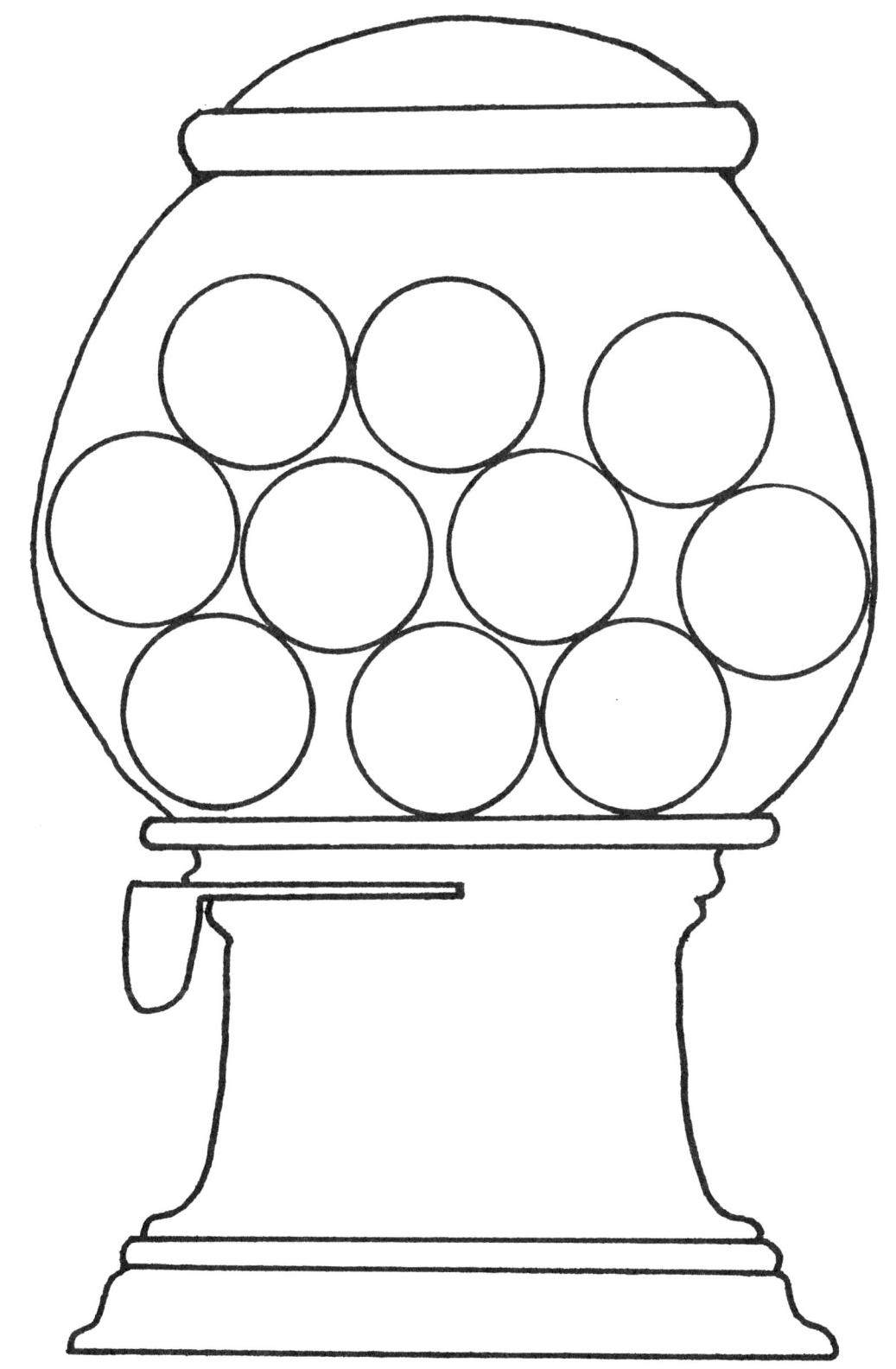

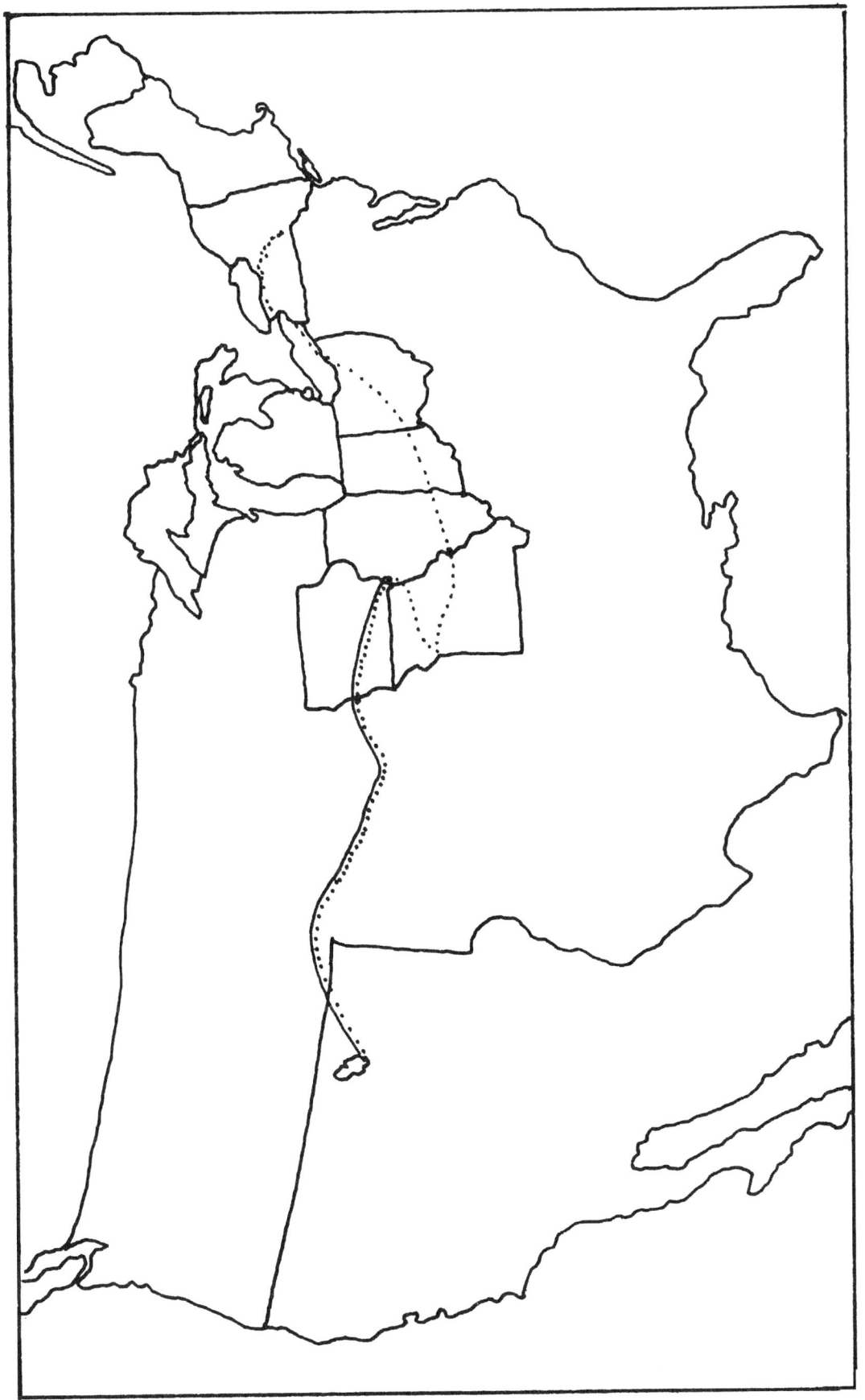

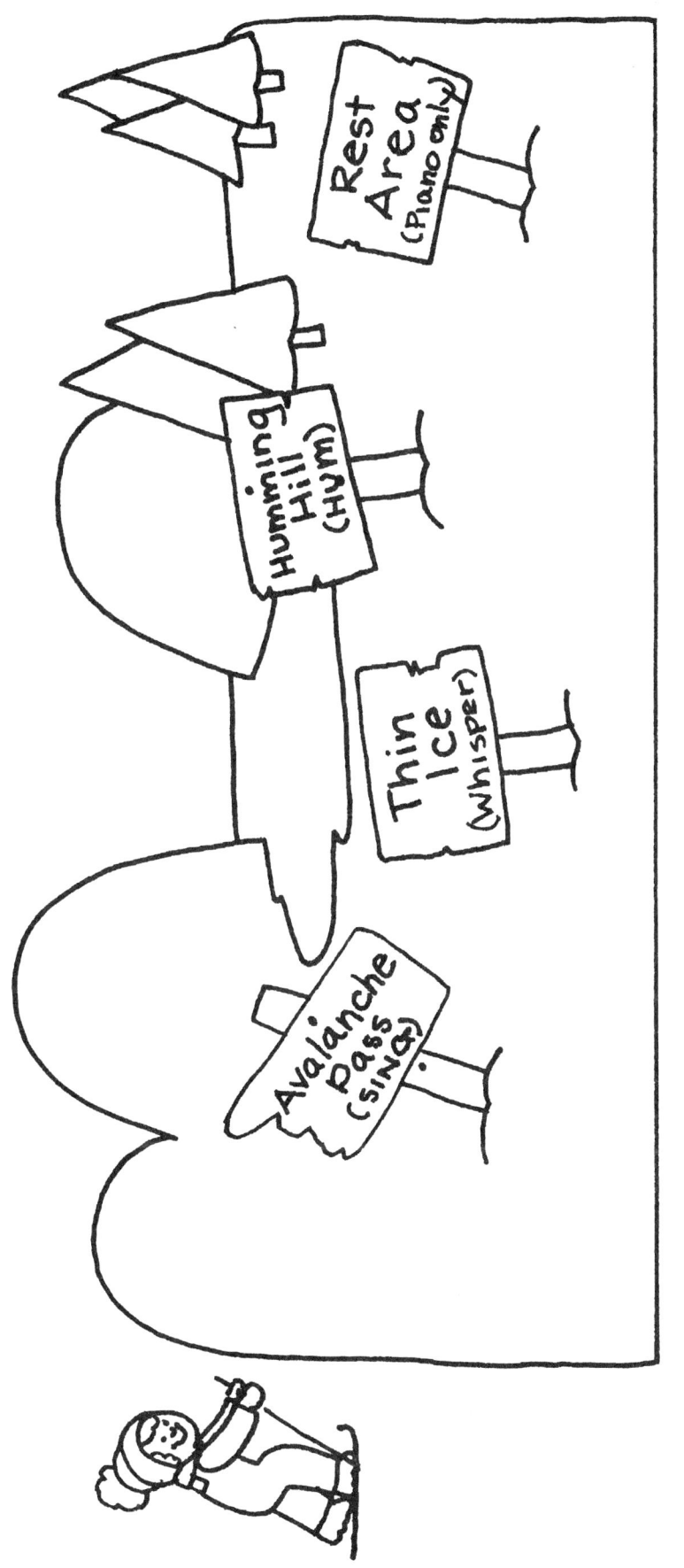

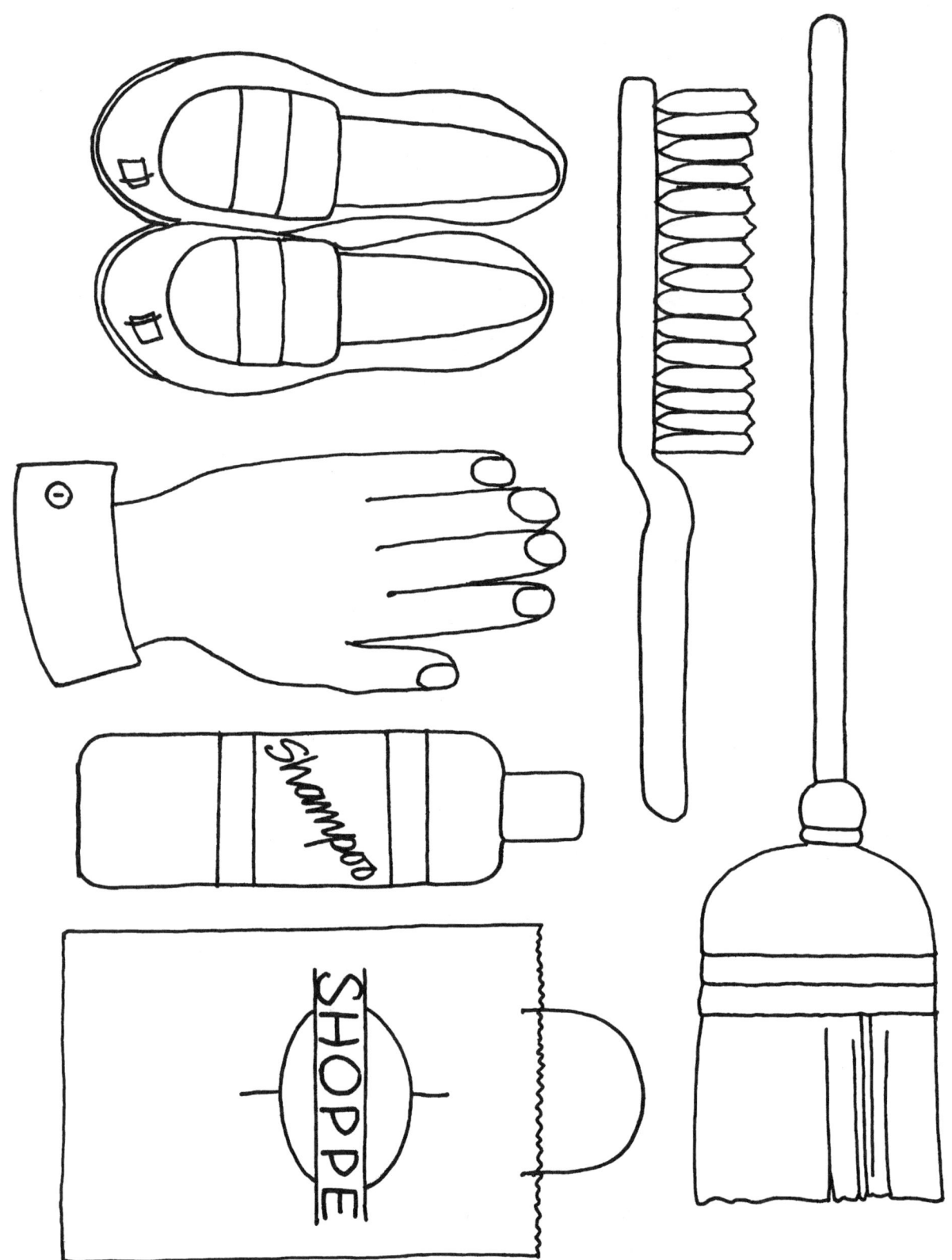

ALPHABETICAL LISTING OF SONG TITLES

A Happy Family	122
A Happy Helper	119
A Prayer	16
A Prayer Song	15
A Song of Thanks	13
Autumn Day	152, 153
Away in a Manger	37
Baptism	72
Beauty Everywhere	144
Because God Loves Me	146
Before I Take the Sacrament	53
Book of Mormon Stories	80
Called to Serve	111
Children All Over the World	11
Come with Me to Primary	157, 158
Covered Wagons	141
Daddy's Homecoming	132
Dare to Do Right	105
Faith	69, 70
Families Can Be Together Forever	115
Family Night	118
Father, I Will Reverent Be	26
Father Up Above	17
Father, We Thank Thee for the Night	8
Fathers	130, 131
Feliz Cumpleaños	171, 172
Follow the Prophet	78, 79
For Health and Strength	14
Friends Are Fun	160
Fun to Do	155
Genealogy—I Am Doing It	65, 66
Go the Second Mile	108
God Is Watching Over All	142, 143
Grandmother	125
Happy, Happy Birthday	173
Happy Song	162
Have a Very Merry Christmas!	42
He Died That We Might Live Again	50
Healthy, Wealthy, and Wise	168
Help Us, O God, to Understand	54
Hinges	167
Home	116
Hosanna	51
How Dear to God Are Little Children	113
How Will They Know?	114
Hum Your Favorite Hymn	100
I Am a Child of God	5
I Am Like a Star	107
I Have a Family Tree	124
I Hope They Call Me on a Mission	110
I Like My Birthdays	74
I Lived in Heaven	6
I Love to Pray	18
I Love to See the Temple	67, 68
I Need My Heavenly Father	12
I Often Go Walking	127
I Pledge Myself to Love the Right	106
I Pray in Faith	10
I Thank Thee, Dear Father	7
I Want to Be a Missionary Now	109
I Want to Be Reverent	25
If You're Happy	163
I'll Walk with You	96, 97, 98
I'm Thankful to Be Me	9
Jesus Is Our Loving Friend	47
Jesus Loved the Little Children	48
Jesus Once Was a Little Child	44, 45
Jesus Said Love Everyone	49
Kindness Begins with Me	99
Latter-day Prophets	92
Listen, Listen	75
Little Jesus	32, 33

Little Lambs So White and Fair	46
Little Pioneer Children	135
Little Seeds Lie Fast Asleep	150
Love One Another	94
Mary's Lullaby	38
Mother, Tell Me the Story	128
Nephi's Courage	81
Oh, Hush Thee, My Baby	41
Oh, What Do You Do in the Summertime?	151
Once Within a Lowly Stable	36
Our Bishop	93
Our Door Is Always Open	156
Our Primary Colors	159
Pioneer Children Sang As They Walked	133
Pioneer Children Were Quick to Obey	134
Quickly, I'll Obey	120, 121
Rain Is Falling All Around	149
Remember the Sabbath Day	103
Repentance	71
Reverence	20
Reverence Is Love	28
Reverently, Quietly	19
Samuel Tells of the Baby Jesus	29
Search, Ponder, and Pray	77
Seek the Lord Early	76
Sing a Song	154
Smiles	164
Springtime Is Coming	148
Teacher, Do You Love Me?	112
The Chapel Doors	104
The Dearest Names	129
The Eighth Article of Faith	89
The Eleventh Article of Faith	90
The Family	117
The Fifth Article of Faith	86
The First Article of Faith	82
The Fourth Article of Faith	85
The Golden Plates	57
The Handcart Song	140
The Hearts of the Children	62, 63, 64
The Lord Gave Me a Temple	101
The Nativity Song	43
The Oxcart	139
The Priesthood Is Restored	60
The Prophet Said to Plant a Garden	147
The Sacrament	52
The Sacred Grove	58, 59
The Second Article of Faith	83
The Seventh Article of Faith	88
The Shepherd's Carol	35
The Sixth Article of Faith	87
The Third Article of Faith	84
The Twelfth Article of Faith	91
The Wise Man and the Foolish Man	169, 170
The Word of Wisdom	102
The World Is So Lovely	145
There Was Starlight on the Hillside	34
This Is God's House	27
This Is My Beloved Son	55
To Be a Pioneer	138
Truth from Elijah	61
Two Happy Feet	165, 166
We Are Different	161
We Are Reverent	21, 22, 23, 24
Westward Ho!	136, 137
When Grandpa Comes	126
When He Comes Again	56
When I Am Baptized	73
When Joseph Went to Bethlehem	30, 31
When We're Helping	123
Where Love Is	95
Who Is the Child?	39, 40